THE WORLD FROM

THE EIGHTH GRADE

From public schools, insane asylums, and juvenile detention facilities, young people give voice to their feelings--though, no one hears--least of all, their parents.

By the same author:

Views From Gold Mountain: History, Memory, Voices

The Calligraphy of San Francisco Chinatown

Chinese Shipping: Its Fall and Rise

THE WORLD FROM THE EIGHTH GRADE

Rabbit Paranoia

Richard Aston

Copyright © 2024 by Richard Aston

Aston, Richard
The World from the Eighth Grade/Richard Aston

wfeg@SixthAvenueBooks.co.uk

Hardback
ISBN: 978-1-7338987-3-7

eBook
ISBN: 978-1-7338987-4-4

BISAC Subject Codes
Social Sciences/Children's Studies, SOC047000.
Language Arts and Disciplines/Writing/Children and Young Adult, LAN005030.
Juvenile Nonfiction/Language Arts/Composition and Creative Writing, JNF029010.

DEDICATION

To the memories of,

Bernice Woo-dip Wong Aston

and

Helen Lai-yun Gan Aston

WITH ACKNOWLEDGMENTS TO:

The hundreds of students I had the privilege of meeting, particularly that unforgettable first class at Martin Luther King School, Sausalito, who taught me so much.

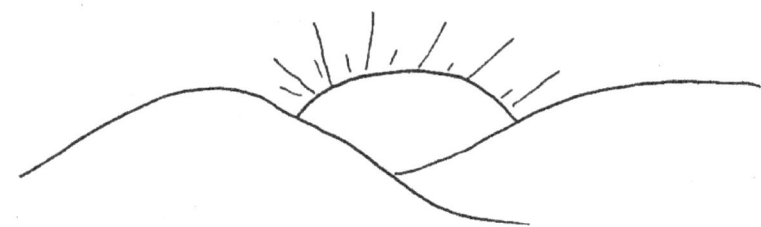

CONTENTS

Acknowledgements   vi
Preface   ix

Part One:
Martin Luther King, Sausalito

Introduction   1
1. The First Assignment   9
2. Social Studies   22
3. "Tupages"   26
4. Mr. Aston   34
5. Class Rules   40
6. Teachers   42
7. Thoughts While in Class   46
8. Books you have read   53
9. Textbooks   58
10. Yesterday   61
11. Today's News   71
12. Thematic Apperception Test   74
13. On the Death of a Seagull   95
14. Who are you?   98
15. Friends   107
16. More Tupages   125
17. The Robot Computer   133
18. Mr. Aston's Mid-Year Report   136
19. The Mind is a Miracle   140
20. Man, What is He?   151
21. Black and White   159
22. The Generation Gap   169
23. Getting Stoned   173
24. Pollution   179
25. The State of the Union   187

26. In the Year 2000	195
27. Mr. Aston's Report Card	213
28. Moratorium Day	219
29. The Flag	226
30. The Grand Jury	236
31. Return to Segregation	253

Part Two:
Agnews State Hospital   255

Part Three:
Oakland Public Schools   261

Afterword   270

****

PREFACE

Toward the end of 1969, I was a graduate student at the University of California, Berkeley, working on a Ph.D. dissertation regarding the Chinese economy, with the expectation of going into government service. One evening a friend who was a teacher at Martin Luther King School, (MLK) in the town of Sausalito, a school in recent headlines for being one of the first in the nation to be racially integrated, called me.

The she wondered if I would help re-write the present eighth-grade social studies curriculum, to better reflect the values of the community. Pleased to be asked, the next Friday afternoon, I drove over to the school to offer my services. I was totally surprised by what followed. The principal, Sidney Walton, (a black man—an important distinction in later developments), came straight to the point. "Since the beginning of the school year in September, five Social Studies teachers have quit. Can you teach? Do you want a job? If so, get to the county education office before they close, and the job is yours."

Driving straight to there, they told me to return Monday morning with proof of education, and a promise to enroll in a teacher training program--then they would issue a provisional teaching credential.

The following Monday, mid-morning, credential in hand, I arrived at MLK. The harried office secretary waved it aside, merely saying "You're in room two." Asking what I was supposed to do, she replied, "Like, do your thing man!"

At 10 o'clock on November 21, 1969, I walked into classroom number two...and found absolute chaos. Although the substitute teacher was showing a film on the political problems of the Middle East, no one was watching. The kids were playing tag, dashing in and out of the room, others, sitting in the usual classroom chairs, were pushing themselves around the room with their feet, while making "choo-choo" noises. Two were sitting on top of a six-foot high cabinet banging their feet against the doors. No one was paying any attention to me.

Seeing a yardstick in a corner, I picked it up and slammed it down on the teacher's desk. With a that sound like a gunshot, the class froze. Silence. Seizing the moment, I bellowed, "Shut up! Find a seat. And sit in it. Or get out and don't come back without your parent or guardian!" Reluctantly, they complied. Continuing, "My name is Richard Aston. You may call me 'Richard,' or 'Mr. Aston,' and I will address you in a similar way. We have eighty-nine days to get you ready for high school, and that is what I intend to do."

Finding some index cards in the desk, I handed them out. "Write your name, and that of your parent or guardian, and their phone number and address. I will be calling each and every one of them, to discuss your progress in school."

Thus began twenty years of teaching….
****

PART ONE

MARTIN LUTHER KING JUNIOR HIGH SCOOL
SAUSALITO, CALIFORNIA

Introduction

Sausalito is a picturesque township nestled on the Bay, a short drive north from San Francisco across the Golden Gate Bridge. The population of about seven thousand is preponderantly white and may be divided into the following socioeconomic groups.

A small group of "old families" who established themselves in Sausalito at the time of the 1906 earthquake. Probably equal in number, is the group of skilled or semi-skilled white workers employed in boat yards, service stations, restaurants, and other businesses.

Other distinct groups are, the "Gate Five" people, (referring to an area of house-boat dwellers), and "hippies" many of whom are involved in the arts or have casual employment.

Before the 1950's, Sausalito was a quiet, picturesque, town, with a couple of small fish restaurants. Within a few years the population boom changed the entire ambiance. Discovered by middle-class, mostly white, professional, people, who found it an easy commute from San Francisco, Sausalito rapidly became a vibrant suburb. In the words of students at the Sausalito's junior high school, the town was rapidly changing.

*****

"The other day I was walking down Bridgeway in Sausalito. It really makes me sick to see all those tourist shops and restaurants. Sausalito is really getting fucked up. All those tourists. You can hardly walk down the street. I wouldn't go there if I didn't know people who lived there. I love to go see all my friends and just stand around talking and having fun, but I really wish they would stop building all those damned buildings. " (Emily Marie).

*****

"Sausalito is a pretty cool place except for all the fucking tourist shops and all the super up-tight residents who, if you have long hair, will hassle you--but usually we're in groups and we can deal with them." (Joe Fork).

*****

"I went downtown tonight and there is a full moon, and everybody is reacting to it. The people in the bars are all ripped off their butts and all of the speed freaks are sitting on the Excelsior Lane stairs singing. Some have pretty good voices.

Sausalito is becoming weirder every year. When I moved here the Bay was reasonably clean and there was not any smog. The tourists came on the weekends, so we would only come out on week days. It worked O.K. Now, there is smog, the water is dirty, there's more cars, roads and people, all week long, the place is so crowded, ik!

There used to be a hole about forty feet deep and about ninety across, it was like an upside down cone. The bottom was full of water and a cocker spaniel that chewed on rocks lived there. They filled it up.

There was a real nice electronics shop little ways from the hole. It had nice people and about a million T.V. sets in a little room fifteen by fifteen. It blew up. There was a hardware store too. It had everything in it. It went out of business because the owner died.

Sausalito then was so much friendlier. There was no traffic lights, narrow streets, and very few cops. Its s really tragic. I guess it couldn't last. (Lief Erickson).

*****

Marin City

Physically separated from Sausalito by an interstate freeway and pedestrian underpass, but politically in the same township, is Marin City. Buit during World War II to house workers from a nearby shipyard, in 1969, Marin City was home to 458 families, 95% of whom were black. While Marin City is physically a pretty community, and in no way conforms to the popular image of a ghetto, it does share many problems with other depressed areas. There is a high degree of unemployment, (more than 50% among males), a lack of facilities (only one small grocery store) and, most importantly, the sense, among the residents, that this, in truth, is a ghetto.

*****

"About life in Marin City. There is almost no place to go in Marin City except like the Boy's Club. There is no big store in Marin City, but it is an all right place. Marin City is a place people go in and out of.

There is nearly nowhere to go. Sometime people may take a walk in the woods and sometimes bike around shooting their B.B. guns.

In the summer I am expecting to get a job, but I remember last year there were no jobs for people fourteen years old. They has cards to get jobs, but the E.O.C. [Equal Opportunity Council] office did not have a lot of money and so they give the girls jobs." (Bob)

*****

"I was just listening to the record called *The Ghetto* and it brought to me something I read. This book was talking about the boys in Marin City, but it didn't say Marin City, they said the boys in the Ghetto.

So now Marin City is called a Ghetto. But I don't think it really is. Just because ninety-nine per cent are black people it doesn't necessarily have to be a Ghetto." (Tamila Shalon).

*****

Within the Marin City community there are social and economic divisions. A major classification is between those who live in the "flats," — high-rise public housing-- and the "pole-house people," residents of private houses built on the slopes of the surrounding hills.

The Forts
Scattered throughout southern Marin County are a number of Army and Airforce installations. The children of servicemen at these bases are allowed to send their children to Sausalito schools.

The Outsiders
Finally, there are a number of families who live outside of the Sausalito school district but send their children into Sausalito either because it is convenient or, more importantly, because [according to their own statements] they "want their children to go to a school where they will meet black children."

Martin Luther King School.
After the establishment of Marin City during the war, lack of school funding, lack of adequate planning, and prejudice, led to the de facto segregation of the white Sausalito schools and the black Marin City schools.

Subsequent to much community action, in 1965 the Sausalito schools were desegregated, probably one of the first school districts in the nation to do so. A school, later named Martin Luther King, was designated to serve grades five through eight.

Thus, MLK serves a very diversified population. One half of the kids are black, mostly coming from the working class, suburban ghetto of Marin City, with a few from the "forts". The white kids can be self-divided into "middle class", "hippies," "forts," and "country," each with different outlook on life.

Politics
Since the school was desegregated the number of white children attending the school had steadily decreased. A major reason for this decline is the fact that many families have withdrawn their children to put them into private schools.

Over the past several years, the school has been a site of periodic problems brought about by the political activities of various community groups. Roughly these are white conservatives, white liberals, black liberals, and black and white radicals. That these political upheavals continue will be seen in the following writings.

The Classes.
Because I had a friend teaching at the school, I was somewhat aware of the structure of the student body at MLK, but it turned out that I was totally unprepared for the attitudes and diversity that I found among the pupils.

The eighth-grade was divided into three groups of twenty- four. These groups were composed as mixed as possible (half boys, half girls, half black, half white, all abilities, and personalities). Their ages ranged from twelve to fifteen, with the average about thirteen and a half, with some advanced because of physical size or maturity. Even physically there was great diversity, from a boy four feet eight and eighty- four pounds, to a girl six feet two and one hundred and fifty pounds.

The range of academic ability in each group was totally unexpected. In each class, about three students were virtually illiterate, their score on the Stanford reading achievement test being "0". On the other hand, one student was reading Thoreau (and not because it was assigned), while another, on the first day of class, inquired if I had ever read *1984,* and asked if I thought; "Winslow, the protagonist, would have succumbed to the social pressures as he did?"

What and how to teach? This was, and is, the question. Many of these children did not have even the most basic of skills, listening, sitting, reading, writing, etc. The California, state mandated, texts, for the eighth grade social studies, far exceeded the ability of a large portion of the class. Furthermore, if you divide the amount of time I had a class per week, by the number of students, it worked out to be at most only a few minutes per week per student.

An over-riding problem was the fact that the kids, almost without exception, were "turned off" from school, how then to turn them back on. In teacher training classes, we were told; "Make your teaching relevant to the kid's lives, take into account their home life, their culture, their ethnic heritage, etc." "Talk about the American Revolution, but make it come alive, show how it relates to life today, get the kids emotionally involved, use role playing"--these were words of advice that were often given; with the postscript, "You'll see, they'll love it."

I made my first mistake by falling into the trap of tinkering with the content of the curriculum and thinking all I really needed was a subject and the right methodology. But, I had not appreciated the degree to which the kids were "turned off", consequently any of the units I attempted to get going flopped. To be sure, some kids were interested enough in a topic to do something about it—talk or read or listen or write—but these were always the same kids that usually demonstrated some sort of positive values (e.g., the value of communication, of progress, of social action), but most kids couldn't have cared less. Perhaps "not caring" isn't the correct term, maybe a more accurate phrase is "the inability to get interested."

This lack of interest, even in the things they claimed interested them most, was brought home when I gave the students permission to play records while doing writing assignments. Rarely was a 45. record played all the way through. Often, after a couple of minutes, someone would say, "I've had enough of that, put something else on." They were bored.

In the classroom, this boredom created within many students a tension that had to be eased by some sort of physical activity, such as continual drumming on the desk or walking around the classroom. Books and magazines were picked up, glanced at, then thrown down, pencils were chewed to bits, and there were constant expressions of impatience.

Part of the problem, was the pupil's perception of time. Perhaps because of the McLuhan electric age, everything must be now, but, whereas this idea has usually meant being aware of what is happening now, living in the present, even relishing each moment, with the students it seemed to be more a position of, "I want time speeded up, I want the future now."

Everything is too slow. Books cannot be read because their ideas are presented at such a snail's pace. Magazines can be flipped through because of the instant image of the photos, but the text is never read. One surprise I had was the response to my question, "What T.V. programs do you watch?" Over half said they didn't much care for T.V. as it was too slow and boring.

So, I abandoned the idea of trying to present social science material in a way that would "turn everyone on," as I felt I could not compete with TV shows every day. But then what to do? I decided that if I wanted to teach, first I'd better find out where the kid's minds were "at." How did they see themselves? How did they see their peers? What, in fact, was going on inside their heads?.

Instead of trying pack their heads with more facts, I decided to concentrate on trying to improve their ability to express the ideas and feelings they already had (preferably in writing). I felt that the increased ability to communicate one's ideas, even if those ideas were not profound, or expressed with grammatical rigor, was of more value to a student than anything else I could attempt.

The responses printed below were gathered over a period of six months. At first they tended to be a little sterile but, as the students and I developed greater rapport, they became more personal and franker. I tried to be as non-threatening as possible, but at the same time let it be understood that I expected the work to be completed. The papers were not graded, nor corrected, a point that caused some hostility among some parents and teachers, but which I felt led to freer expression.

As a result, most of the writing is imaginative, and an honest expression of feeling. Furthermore, I challenge any adult to enter a cold classroom at eight-thirty on a dark, wet, winter, Monday morning, and in the next fifty minutes write, on demand, a beautiful essay on the meaning of life. It seemed to me that, having gained, at least in part, the tool of writing, many of these students experimented in expressing their thoughts and feelings more precisely. Any mistakes or lapses in good taste (to put it mildly) should be seen in this light.

It is not possible to include here even a quarter of all the pages turned in. Therefore, there was the problem of selection. This was not done with any methodological rigor and was purely subjective. I chose those writings that seemed representative of the whole or expressed a point particularly well. As a result, the writings of students who were more adept at communication are in the majority. However, this still gives a good picture of the values of the majority of the students, as the words of articulate students often reflected the feelings of those less proficient in writing them down.

In editing individual pieces of writing, errors were seldom corrected, although some were tidied up (one twenty page paper was a single sentence), in most cases, the original was kept to show the writer's ability and thought processes.

In order to encourage the freedom of expression, pen names were used to hide identity of the writers from other teachers, parents, and peers. Also, when the writing mentions another student that name was changed. However, the names of teachers and administrators are as in the original. There seemed no point in in obscuring their identity as the comments were usually made quite publicly--at school board meetings, press conferences and on the radio.

ASSIGNMENTS

1. *The First*

Please tell me something about yourself, your family, your likes, your dislikes, — anything that will help me get to know you a little better. What is your favorite T.V. program, food, hobbies-- anything at all.

"I find these kind of papers make me feel uneasy' and make me feel as though you are nosey. What will I say? Well, I'm very happy, I'm living, and my past doesn't really matter. Please have us write compositions that are more interesting (I've written these about three times in the past two years). Well, anyways, if I go on like this I'll probably get in trouble, I sometimes get very pessimistic, but it never lasts very long. " (Rabbit Paranoia).

*****

"I am now fourteen and go to Martin Luther School. I have lived in Marin City all of my life. All the while I was in school and until I got in the seventh grade I would cry every time the teacher would say something to me. I didn't know why, I just did.

All the while we lived in Marin City we lived in these ragged houses on top of the hill. Then we moved to these old houses down in the flats. To find out more about Marin City and how it looked while I was growing up I think you should buy the book called *Marin City, U.S.A.*, and if you would like to buy one they cost two dollars. " (Tamila Shalon).

*****

"I live in Sausalito. I'm a Gemini. Geminis are so crazy, as you see. I live in a big gray house. We are so rich we don't know what to do." (The Gemini).

*****

"I'm fourteen, black and my name is Yolanda. I was born in Winnsboro, Louisiana, in March of 1956. March the third to be exact. I can't actually say that I'm positive of my date or parents, but who can be? They say they are relatives. I look like my parents, so I believe them. Belief is sureness in this case, to me. I feel that people feel to me as a friend but let's face it you can't live nowhere in this world where you are liked by everyone. Somebody will dislike you for some reason if no more than the way you turn your head. That's just the way things are. You can say the world is what you make it. If you want people to admire, or like you, you should act in the way that they will.

My future? Well, it can't tell. It's not mine to predict, but I've planned it. I would like to be an elementary school teacher. The kindergarten, 1st, 2nd.or 3rd. I do plan to go to college and get a Ph.D., if that is not possible, a master's degree. Marriage? Of course, I feel that being married, raising a family is part of living. I had thought of getting married in '76. I will graduate in '74 and will have had two years of college. I plan to continue after marriage, but if not I could get a job; secretary somewhere because I'm taking typing, not going to stop until perfection, but with the top typers or be the best. No children until we're established and have something to offer them.

Like I said I'm Black. Black people are people who should always want to succeed and not fail. We've always been behind. Letting the white man blow our mind. He brought us over here to his country and made us slaves. Made us come in his back door and shine his shoes, clean his house, all we were doing was "Kissing his Ass!" We've moving up. Not trying to say that the black race is the only one that's right. NA! What I'm saying is that we've been rejected. Everyone with the dark skin isn't black. Some are colored and white. Your color is on your skin, but the color that counts is in your mind. I'm Black. I strive to succeed. I try. Sometimes I jive, but I'm still young, it's all a part of youth.

I put my name on this paper because I feel I said nothing to offend no one. These are my feelings. I expressed myself and don't mind who know it." (Yolanda).

*****

"When I wake up in the morning I don't feel very well sometimes. I may wake up and just sit on the side of the bed very drowsily then start making up my bed. I'll do about eight push-ups if I feel like it then get some clothes on and soon stagger to the bathroom. Get a little six square inch towel, run some hot water on it, rub it with some soap and then rub it on my face very briskly, then I may start waking up slowly and then brush my teeth. Then I may start getting hollered at from downstairs asking where the comb is, if I seen it." (Jake Brown).

*****

"There are four people in my family. It doesn't matter who they are. When I finish with school I want to be a poet and an author. I hate private property. I'm going to own as little as possible once I leave home. I'll live on government property and live off the land as much as possible. I don't like T.V., and it doesn't matter which movie star I like. In some ways I would like to be like Thoreau because he had some of the ideals I would like to have and some of the values." (Adam).

*****

"Marin City is a small ghetto. Most of Marin City houses are little. The pole houses are the only ones big enough for people in Marin City. My family house is little. We have an up-stairs and down-stairs, but both are little. There are six kids in our family plus my mother and three dogs, two birds, two bicycles and lots of toys. My mother would like to get a bigger and better home for all of us. My mother sleeps downstairs as she wants us to have a room before she does because she is so sweet hearted. When we have company it gets so crowded and there is not much room to move around the house. Our yard is little. My mother tries to plant flowers in the garden and there is not enough room for us to play. The kitchen is so little only about two persons can move around in it with food.

I have to get up at 5:30, get dressed, cook breakfast for everybody in my family, set the table and call everyone to come and get it. All of that time takes about fifty minutes. Then I eat and put all the dishes away. After I do all that I am so tired. Then I got to get my hair curled and then take my brother to school, fix my lunch, make up my bed and by that time it is 8:30.

When I catch the bus to go to school some people on the bus I don't like. I can't get along with them and they can't get along with me, so I just don't pay no attention to them. But they take advantage of me. They tease me and make fun of me. They do that because they know I am going to get mad, so they keep on teasing me, but I don't get mad.

Now we are at school they are pushing and making noises and trying to scare me and some of them do. Because I am shy and timid in class they make fun of me. It's always the black students not the white students.

I would rather be with all white students in a class for a better education because black people play around too much and don't complete their assignments. I am not saying white people are better than black people, they are not different from black — only the color. But it does not matter why you let race bother you. All it can do is get you down where the white people want you to be. This is a hard world to live in. I can't live in it because I am down. Once I get up I am back down again. WHITE IS OVER BLACK!" (Prudence).

*****

"I am thirteen years old. I am not smart, and I am not dumb, just in between. I don't like people to try to make me do something. If I am to do it I will do it on my own. I don't like to be pushed by no one and when you send notes home on me it doesn't bother me. I know that I will be fussed at, but I don't mind because all I do is shine right on. If you push me too hard I will act just like I don't hear or see you." (Puddingtang).

*****

"The world is coming to an end, but I have liked, loved, hated and died. Jumped thru, threw through, grew moo, jingle bells, jungle bells, rub a rubber tree he like to... Oh, oh, oh, steak, potatoes, chocolate cream cake, pecan pie, garlic bread, chicken, ice cream, cookies, coke, chew, swallow, digest, exlax, pimples???" (Joe Fork).

*****

"I dig small mechanisms (i.e., watches). I like cats. I like certain dogs. I like racoons. I like grass. I like good teachers (I hope you are a good teacher). I like writing with pens. I like to travel, except I don't (no money). I like talkative grandparents. I like a lot of things. I like Mt. Tam. I like Stinson Beach. I like sandals (but ain't got none). I like colors. I like some books. I like warm blankets. I like Simon and Garfunkel. I like good music. I like clean hair. I like Mrs. White. I like Mr. Flores (Mr. Sidhu too). I hope I'll like Mr. Aston. I like printing. I like sleeping. I like tacos without hot sauce. I like Odd Bodkins. I like Donovan. I like the Stones, Turtles and Beatles. I like Arlo Guthrie. I like California. I like Easy Rider. I like KSAN. I like recorders. I like guitars. I like pianos and flutes. I like Niell. . I like thinking about things I like. I like Martin Luther King School. I like Christmas vacation. I like cats again, except when they shit in the house. I like cold, dry weather. I like clean teeth. I like suede. I like sweaters. I like Doc Savage. I like Gandalf Bilbo too. I like Up the Down Staircase (but I've forgotten it). I like daisies. I like to paint. I like homemade foods. I like clean clothes. I like dirty clothes. There's plenty more but, as I said before, I like sleeping and I want to now. Good night. " (Karen).

*****

"I hate writing or reading autobiographies that start like, "I was born in New York Muni Hospital and learned to walk at one and a half" or anything like that. My opinion of life is usually that I'd rather live a short life and have a good time than have a long life and be afraid of everybody. I get pissed off rather quickly and don't get along with many people. I would like to be Nixon because he can murder people legally." (Leif Erickson).

*****

"In my family there are five people. I don't have a favorite T.V. program. Its none of your business what I do after school. I don't have a favorite person. Football and girls." (Ian).

*****

"I like people and I like clothes. I am a very nice young man and I like field trips. The good point about me is that if I see somebody jumping on somebody else and they don't want to fight I will try and stop it. The bad point about me is if I get mad I won't listen to nobody." (Johnny).

*****

"I live in the ghetto which is Marin City. It is one of the richest in the country, but I don't like it. I don't put up a front. I love to meet different people and when someone says something to me I say something back to them. My feelings are hard to solve. I think of my homework if I don't do it and my conscience always tells me, "You better do your homework," and I say to myself, "I don't want to do it." So, I don't do it.

And I am groovy and up-tight and out-a-sight. I dug on teachers and that's all I got to say. Right-on, Soul Brother and Sister." (Little Green Man), (a girl).

*****

"The main thing that goes on in my mind is the world. I go to school, come into class and learn about people starving in Asia. I learn about pollution, war and greed, and then I learn about all the letters I can write to the president about all the problems and how little they do. And then I'm told I have the whole world at my doorstep. Well, I don't want it in my lap. I'm sick of feeling guilty anytime I throw out a chicken bone.

Of course, it wasn't always like this. My feelings are recent. When I first felt depressed I tried to laugh it off, but now I can't. Actually, it's not hearing all the things wrong that makes me mad, it's that I can do so little about it—at least things that would work. I can protest, write letters, but that doesn't work at all.

But enough of the world. Things that make me happy are getting few and far between, like Christmas, for instance. I used to love to open presents, but now it's not fun. I personally hope it's just a stage in life and it's going to be better later on, but right now things are going wrong." (Potassium Nacnud).

*****

"I've lived in Marin City for twelve years. I was born 1956, June 30. I'm male and negro and my religion is Catholic, and my name is Davis, Roger C. and I go to Martin Luther King School in Sausalito. I've been going to this school now for three and a quarter years and I think it was a little better than the last' time I was here. Now it's starting to progress better in my last year. I don't care if I'm white or Black I'm a young man, and thats what counts. I'm what I want to be, not what I have to be. Actually, I think at the starting of my life time I always wanted to be what the other men were. Now I'm acting like I want to be. Pressure is leaving me and I'm going on.

I think poetry is doing your own thing--expressing yourself. I think being a poet shows that you are progressing instead of running track backwards when there is always a different direction. So, stay, and think, then go a step further, but you always stay a step ahead of yourself. No matter what, be cool, until it gets to that you are caught in a trance between light and dark, until you finally relax and let go and stuck between God and man, you can't go no farther. Suspended animation rather than the known, as caught in the walls of time." (Roger).

*****

"I am a very strange person, and I don't know what's wrong with me. Sometimes, when I am listening to music, I get that I love it so much that I start crying. I know it's a pretty stupid thing to do, but I can't help it. "And a rock feels no pain, and an island never dies." I just heard this, and I really love this line.
I love to make things: earrings, necklaces, just little things, and keep them or give them to my friends. One other thing I love is being alone, because when I'm alone I can do anything I want. I am just

beginning to figure myself out, but it will take me a long time because I am a very complicated person. These are some words I made up.

> Someday there'll be
> a love so true
> That we shall hide
> no truth from you
> Oh God, my Lord.
> And if that day
> should ever come
> You shall know first
> You'll sit and rule
> A peaceful world
> That has no hate
> No lies, no war
> Just love and faith
> To you I'll bring
> this world some day
> Some day, Some day.
> I LOVE LIVING." (Janie).

*****

"I think my idea is that I don't have much about myself. All I've done my whole life is waste my time doing nothing but play around in school. So, I'm going to work harder and study harder and think about the future and what I'm going to do the rest of my life. So, this is my opinion about myself." (Dude).

*****

"I've lived in Marin City for eight years now. Marin City is a very cool town to me cause Marin got what it takes cause there are some very cool people here. Marin is the best place I ever lived in. My age is twelve years old. I have a large family and there is about fourteen of us. I have five boyfriends. They are all cousins, and they all know I go out with each of them." (Francis).

*****

"The Bad Basis of My Life. It started back in 1955 when my mom and dad got it on. A year later I was born. I'll try and tell you everything. I'm semi-lazy and I'm pretty selfish and I tend to go my own way. Sometimes I'm very demanding and I like to conquer things and I don't usually give them back unless they are taken away from me. I expect more out of people than they expect out of me. I'm very short tempered and always want to get even with people." (Ho Chi-minh Lennon).

*****

"My middle name is, "What?" I like paint, painting, being painted, finger paint, canvas paint, house paint, car paint and girls. I dislike authoritarians, dictators, capitalism, government, *Civics in Action* [the required textbook] and bad paintings. When I get out of school I want to be: grown up, a girl, a rock, some water, dead, young, educated, Freud, a match, a lit match, a blown out match, a spring, a water spring, a wet spring, a dry Fall, a clean summer, a dirty winter, a sexy novel, a Greek God, agreed God, a creek dog, assistant to an ass (Ph.D.), a winner, a loser, a fink, a pot head, a coke bottle, a coke sniffer, a coke sniffed, some cocaine, some pot, a stop watch, a watch, a stopped watch, a watched stop, a watched stop sign, a stop sign." (Washington Irving).

*****

"I don't know what to write about, but I will anyway. If I could trust you completely I would write about my personal life. But, since I can't, I won't. So that is just too bad for you. You won't learn about my life if I can help it." (Mark).

*****

"My name is Edith. There are seven persons in my family, two brothers, two sisters and my mother and father. I want to be a telephone operator like my older sister. My favorite T.V. program is Room 222. I would like to be Doris Day. My favorite sport is hockey. My favorite food is chicken, and my favorite class is art. My favorite candy is Hershey. My favorite ice cream is rocky road.

My favorite place is Palm Springs although I have never been there." (Edith).

*****

"I can not tell you how many are in my family, and I don't intend to." (Franklin).

*****

"There are six people in my family. We all look alike. I am the only one that does not look alike. I want to be a boxer so I can go around and hit people in the mouth." (Allan).

*****

"Well, myself I think of a young man who is trying to go up in life. You hear about wars, killing, and rapes it make me want to think what to live for. Some boys I know younger than me take dope. Getting off that into my likes and dislikes. I like football and I hate baseball. I like sex. I hate dope. In getting off that, what I think most of the time is helping the black people of the ghettoes I think about getting better job, better houses."
My Poem
Black boy, White boy
White boy, White boy, were will you go?
Black boy, Black boy, I don't know." (Eddie).

*****

"I am very beautiful and wear my hair in a natural. I have dark brown hair that matches my brown eyes. (Love Bug).

*****

"I was born on July 16, 1956, in the State of California. My childhood was up-tight, and my parents kept it that way. As I grew up my life differed from the other children in the neighborhood. My parents were very cool, they didn't yell and scream at us because we broke things. All my mother would say was, "Be careful next time." Both were alright.

When I became five I began to realize that life wasn't just a house of dolls. Growing up in Marin City there were not many ambitions that one could have. I always thought that reading was an important one and to get somewhere you have to know how to read.

Getting along with people can sometimes be a problem for me, if they don't like me then I won't be able to get along with them. Speaking to people is not a problem at all for I will speak to a person even if he or she doesn't speak to me.

I don't have much to talk about. I can tell you are nosey. I dig reading for it is cool, dig? You know it's up-tight and out-of-sight." (Somon Marie).

*****

"I, Simon, am a person. I am interested in the world around me and the events that shape it. At the present time I am interested in becoming a lawyer and working in the field of civil rights. I am already in county government as a member of the Marin County Youth Commission. I represent the seventh, eighth and ninth grade.

I have been involved in other things. I have done some work for the Cora Foundation (I talked to a group of interns about the transfer system between Mill Valley and Sausalito and about M.L.K. school). I ran for student body president and lost. I am now involved in the student council as a student advisor. I was once one of the one hundred Marin County representatives to the Governor's State House Conference." (Simon).

*****

"I like people, whites too. I do not like to talk much, and I do not like to write." (Penny).

*****

"I dislike a lot of things in this country, including the people in the government. I think my life is going by really fast and I want to do something worthwhile with myself. I keep saying that I'm going to do things, but I never get things done. I just keep putting it off until the next day. But I can't do that anymore. Once I get into high school I'm going to have to start doing things.

I get mad too easily and I start yelling. I don't like getting mad. I am a Leo. The sun is my ruler and I rule over the heart.

I am for the Indians to get Alcatraz for $24 (or less; they should get it free because it's their land anyways).
I go on all the peace marches on Moratorium days." (Emily Marie).

*****

"When I finish school I would like to go to the smallest island in the ocean." (Vouix).

*****

"I like boys
I like to talk
I hate war
I hate social science
I hate math
I hate language arts
I hate home ec.
I hate science
I hate art
I hate music
I hate library
I hate P.E.
I hate special periods
I hate school, period.
My sign is Capricorn
I hate everybody in the world except:
Becky Mantele, my little sister my dog and cat
Marilyn Edward and Sherry
and I also hate:
principals
principles
students
War
I want the establishment
to bring home the boys.
Not one more dead in Vietnam.
My interest:

To get grass legalized." (Suzi Mantele).

*****

"The first thing I don't like is you." (Bettina).

*****

"My name is Xathier X. Zeus. I don't know what I want to do. Maybe a dope peddler or a secret agent or a billionaire. I might settle for a multi-millionaire. A dope peddler because they are supposed to be sick in the head. A secret agent because they never can get killed, and the other two because they have an easy life. I'd like to be God because he's kind of weird.

My favorite sport is beating up rocks with lead pipes. It relieves my tension. My favorite food is ear wax. I like to watch pebbles grow into strong masculine or feminine rocks. I like preparing for marriage because it so thrilling." (Xathier X. Zeus).

*****

"There are seven people in my family and when I leave school I would like to go home and sleep and if there is anything else you would like to know see me." (Julie).

****

2. Assignment: Social Studies.

It appeared that few junior high school students had any understanding of the content of social studies. Often they believed that "social studies" is synonymous with history, and history is memorizing dates. Hence the following assignment. The majority of the replies were of the nature, "I don't know" but some were quite sophisticated.

Assignment for Today
1. What is the meaning of the words, "social studies"?
2. Why do you think you are required to take social studies?
3. What do you think you should be able to do as a result of taking this social studies class?

"To me it means work." (Shirley).

*****

"To learn about what happened in the past but I get sick and tired of hearing about George Washington and Abraham Lincoln. Out of all the teachers we had they never mentioned none of our race. All they were teaching us about is Goldilocks and the Three Bears." (Little Green Man).

*****

"I don't really know. I guess it's so you know all the things that Americans have done (and they haven't done anything good yet)." (Emily Marie).

*****

"Because I need to know something about this old world." (Fritz the Cat).

*****

"To know what we got into." (Mao Nixon).

*****

"Talk intelligently about whats happening now, not what happened two or three hundred years ago. Know something about why whats happening is happening and be able to try and change it. (My country right or wrong, if right to keep it right, if wrong to set it right.) We should know about our rights. We should use our rights. The study of social life or societies from the past, present and future is what I think it should mean. It seems to mean history." (Washington Irving).

*****

"I think I should know about the outside world, learn about the problems of other peoples, and be able to do something about these problems. I don't want to know what causes revolutions I want to be able to help them. I want to look into specific instances not just any one." (Dusty).

*****

"Walk around town saying the dates of famous happenings. But, if you will change from the war to current events I will not go around like that, O.K.?" (Roberts).

*****

"It means the kinds of people and the countries they live in. It includes the government and problems of the country. Social studies deals with the social aspects of people. I should be able to organize any kind of group, know how to make it work, and have a working government if needed. I should be able to know my rights as a citizen and know what I can and can not do. I should be able to know how to conduct a group so that it can help today's society, or other societies, become better ones.

 Because it increases your knowledge of the world around you and gives you insight as to how things are run in other countries as well as our own. In the long run it gives you an idea as to how you can improve your own country." (Wildflower Weed).

*****

"To me I think that you ought to be teaching us about things that we don't know, like what is going to happen in the future, and what would happen if all the wars stop, what would people do. I think that we should know how to go up to a person and tell them what you think and see what he has to say about it. But to be fair I like the way you are teaching the social science classes. I like the way you let the student pick out the subject that they would like to study, and to me that is understanding the student, and I like the way you are teaching this social science class." (Check).

*****

"It means the regular social life having to do with people in other countries or in pioneer life when George Washington the father of our country was alive. The past, present and future." (Confucius).

*****

"So, you can better understand what's happening in life." (Joe Fork).

*****

"To hear of other people's problems and how we can keep from getting these problems and if we do, how to overcome these problems." (Maria).

*****

"History? History is a thing of the past. If you want to know history. You have to go back. That is no good. Because you can't deal with the things you normally should. Economics? Economics is a right-on thing. Getting your money and giving it back again. Dealing with money is almost everyone's bag. Cause if you got money you go buy you some rags." (Tony Jackson).

*****

"Social studies are about people. How people live, work, and entertain themselves. Where people live, work and entertain themselves. I don't think you can learn this in a classroom. I think you ought to be, "where it's at." (Eleanor Hume).

*****

"I think it means studying about everything and everybody. Because we have to learn these things. One day we might visit a country we're studying and then we'll know more. (Lynn).

*****

"It is the study of the past, present and it is the study of mountains, rivers, famous people, great lakes, lagoons, and oceans." (Jake Brown)

*****

"To do what we are supposed to do, such as know the Bill of Rights. To go out and live with our community. To go out and cope with the other fellow man. To go out and get what you want and fight for what you want, and to do it right." (Dude).

*****

"To not be prejudiced. To not take this bullshit about how beautiful our country is and how backward all other countries are. To be a liberal. To keep an open mind." (Xathier X. Zeus).

*****

"Because the teachers want us to know about the past." (Hal).

*****

"To learn of the many people in ancient times so maybe you might be interested in it." (Confucius).

*****

"We're supposed to know how to do our thing when you get out of this funky class. And we're also supposed to know our past, present, and if we're lucky, future." (Suzi Mantele).

*****

"You should know the Bill of Rights. And I should know about the Declaration of Independence and know a lot about the British wars and how we won independence." (Kimberly).

*****

"I should be able to turn my homework in on time. I should be able to write the Bill of Rights, We the People, and the Declaration of Independence. I should be able to do anything that deals with social science." (Doris).

*****

"I don't really know." (Pimpy).

3. Assignment: Two pages of writing every week.

"Tupages" as they came to be called, started by my stealing an idea from. Daniel Fader's *Hooked on Books*. Each student was required to turn in at least two pages (or "tupages" as it came to be called) of writing each week. The pages could be on anything, and I didn't care what sort of language they used, nor about spelling or grammar. The pages would not be shown to anyone and, if when finished they thought they had written something too personal, even I wouldn't read it. If they couldn't think of anything to write, they could copy out of a book.

The initial response was one of perplexity over the word "anything". The students were conditioned to the idea that in a social science class one writes about American history and, after dozens of inquiries asking: "Can I write a story?" or "Can I write a poem?" I found myself shouting "Anything! Anything!"

After the kids became acclimatized to the idea they really could write anything, there was a period when the language became absolutely foul-- usually criticizing me-but the novelty soon faded. Actually, I'm sorry it did because, for one or two kids on the border of illiteracy, it was the only time they really got enthused over putting something on paper.

Also, a significant number of kids took me at my word and wrote anything—nonsense syllables, numbers, names—often in huge letters and with tremendous margins. One kid even figured out a way of filling a page by holding two pencils together, so he wrote two lines at once. Others consistently copied their two pages from a book. I had mixed feelings about those who obviously did anything just to get by, often feeling I was being "taken," although I had said "anything." But then, I thought, every once in a while, even these students occasionally tried to express highly personal feelings.

The same applies to copying. A number of teachers were horrified, saying this taught the students to steal. I disagreed. There was never any attempt at deception, as the kid would say, "I couldn't think of anything to say, so I copied." Fader remarked that, in his experience, forty-two pages of copying was the most before a student wrote an original line. I was more fortunate, spates of copied work from the students who did the most copying were frequently interspersed with original work.

As for grammar and spelling, several teachers and parents were furious over my lack of concern. All I can say is that when a teenage boy, who can barely write, makes the fantastic effort of pouring out thirty pages about his emotional problems and sexual fears, it would be criminal for me to criticize him because the pages consisted of just one sentence and the spelling was almost indecipherable.

"This is my two paged, this is my two pages, this is my two……. (Edward Smith).

*****

"Wow! I think its really wild that we are supposed to write two pages or more on anything we want. Its the greatest idea. Its now ten to eleven and if I don't stop writing now I'll never get up in the morning. Well, now I have to think of a subject. This is going to be difficult, seeing that I am very tired. About the only time I can write something like this is at night. I just finished watching Marcus Welby till eleven and then there was thunder and lightning, and then my clock wouldn't work, which amounts to my being tired.

This is a very weird thing to do, write in a journal like this. I was wondering what your reasoning was behind it. I thought that we were supposed to study about civil wars, world wars, and stuff like that. Aren't we? I know that I don't know anything about them and when I get to Tam Hi I'm going to be very dumb (which, by the way, I am not, yet!). You'll have to excuse all of my mistakes because I'm in a hurry to finish, because its due tomorrow. (There just went a bang of thunder!) End." (Wildflower Weed).

*****

"I really don't feel like writing these two pages today. I'm tired and have a headache. If anybody talks it hurts more. I'm tired of these days when we just sit here doing nothing. Everybody likes it better when there's a class discussion or something. When there's not, you just sit here getting lazy, not knowing what to do. When nobodys in here I don't know what to say when someone talks to me.

I don't think I'll ever get these two pages done with. The pages get longer and longer. I don't even see why we have to write these. There's no point to it. I feel like screaming. Its good to scream you know, especially when you're all fed up with everything. I hate it when these boys in this class come over to talk about the dumbest things. I don't know what to say to them. Have you ever been to Manchester, England or to Sutton, England? I was just wondering. Why is there so many dumb people in this class?

The boys especially. Not all, just some. I'm really in a bad mood today. Especially after Mrs. Hinton's class. I think I need glasses and Mrs. Hinton makes us read and then I get headaches. Why do people always talk unnecessarily and then I get another headache. Don't grade this on what it looks like and spelling. Maybe my headache comes from not eating. All I eat now is two bowls of rice a day because I'm too fat. I really get discouraged when I'm fat and I try to lose weight and I don't. (Valerie Valias).

*****

"Like I said, I hate writing two pages, but I have to catch up someway. What I really need is someone with a whip making me work. I wish I could have done something like crocheting two pages.

I want to go to Europe someday. I want to go to Italy and see the Sistenth Chapel (that's not spelled right) and The Prado in Spain to see the "Garden of Delights". I already have a reproduction of it. Its about the size of a big poster. I would also like to go to Russia. Some friends of ours went there and they tried to give a maid a tip and she wouldn't except it. Absolutely no one excepts a tip anywhere there." (Maria).

*****

"I went to the Quicksilver show. The music was good but I was a little depressed. It was too hot. A man offered me a piece of acid, but I declined. It was the prettiest' shade of purple I've ever seen. I'm listening to music now and relaxing. I met a kid with an ounce and a half of grass pollen. I've got a sunburn. Caps in caps in bottles with caps in the bottle. Ah, Woody Guthrie. Snap.

I've gotta grow up a little. I've gotta have a Bar- Mitzva for real. Oh, I've gotta come down a little. Sober up and out. Hitchhike. Leave. Let go. Grow musclegs in my hand and in my head. Live. Eat. And make my belle stiff. And I, Adam, do hereby solemnly swear that I won't take any dope until the weekend. The next weekend.

I'm just a writing right here and listening to music and I'm getting tired of writing but I'm punishing myself by forcing myself to write even if it kills you because I'm "hi" and very guilty and doing stupid writing tricks and writing what I shouldn't write. And I'm sleepy but bear with it 'cause someday it'll be worth it. Every fight I ever had with my father. Every promise I broke. Every thought I ever had and every word I ever wrote is gonna be worth it. 'Cause I'm gonna be the writer, poet and maybe singer. And we're all gonna win. We're gonna get what we want cause we're right and they're wrong. And someday I'll be the best at one thing. Someday, no matter how small, I'm going to be the very expertly, most, best at this one thing (at least). Someday...no wait, something I do will always remain and I'll always be in these circumstances no matter how much I don't want to. Oh shit, I want to do something right now and I don't know what. Maybe sleep." (Adam).

*****

"At home we have these seven neurotic cats. One is mentally retarded, one once weighed over twenty pounds, one has had nineteen kittens in the past year, one female falls in love with every boy she sees, one boy cat walks around the house constantly, meowing as loud as he can, and the other two haven't taken over the neuroticism as of yet.

It all started one day when this cat followed my sister home. We had these other two cats who were always running around the house acting crazy, and this one cat acted so gentle and petite we called him Dame. A couple of years later he was the biggest cat in the neighbood, weighing twenty-two pounds and always getting in fights. Once he had his ear torn in half and it still is. I could go on and write ten pages about him.

About five years later this little girl cat had kittens and then later she had more kittens, then her kittens had kittens, and then she had more kittens in a year. Before we knew it cats were all over the place. A little while later distemper hit and three or four died. My Mom took some to the Humane Society. Finally, we had this black cat.

We have this mentally retarded cat who is pure black. This cat tries to go up and kiss dogs. He doesn't know whether he is a cat, dog, human, bird, girl, boy, a baby, a big cat, or just what. We have another cat who is a sex maniac. He is black and the dumbest cat. He used to walk around the neighborhood meowing, so we had him altered. We have this other cat, who is striped. This cat tries to seduce all the males. If we don't watch out she'll have kittens in just a little while. The other cats, Romeo and Juliet are just kittens and haven't started acting like Romero and Juliet yet and my Mom sure hopes they never do." (Valerie Valias).

*****

"When you're talking to a strawberry its not always easy to stand on fifteen feet especially when you're supposed to be tutoring Sir Genius in fractions at one o'clock and you've been looking forward to it for a long time and now I won't be able to tutor him because I came home. DAMN IT.

Let me see. I have to write about ten pages for Mr. Aston, so I'd better think of something to write. I wonder why Malcolm wasn't in school today. Thats it. School. What am I talking about????????? Just forget it.

There is a little nest in the hedge in front of our house. I go there to look at it all the time. I really like it. It has two eggs in it and its really nice.

I also like things like: Bob Dylan and thinking about things. I've got about one and a third pages now, but I don't know what else to write to make it two pages. I know, I'll write a poem. But what about?

Cold War, Cruel War, Bloody War, Talking War, Killing War?

I don't know what to write. How many times have I started these dumb two pages out like that? I don't know. I usually start it out like that because I always wait until around 11:00 Tuesday night before its due to write it. And so I want to hurry up and write it because I am tired and it is hard for me to get up at 7:45 in the morning. A lot of times I don't get tired at night because I like to stay up late, but I make up for it by not wanting to get up in the morning.

I think I'll write a little about myself. First I have to tell you that I don't mean completely all of what I wrote last week. I was very mad. and didn't feel like writing. I was mad at you mainly for a few of the reasons that I explained last week. Well enough of that.

O.K., one of my problems is that I find it very difficult to get mad at a person in their presence. I mean, I can't tell them in person. If I were very close to somebody then I probably would be able. But seeing that I am not very close to anybody I can't get mad, or rather show my emotions too easily.

Another thing is that nobody listens to me. I'm talking about at school, not at home. Do you know what I did? A couple of weeks ago I wrote about three pages of stuff for this thing then tore them up because: 1., It was not completely true; 2., It was too, too

personal; 3., I wouldn't have been able to show it to anybody; Dumb wasn't it?
(Wildflower Weed).

*****

"Henry Anderson Henrry Anderson Henry Anderson Henry Anderson Henry Anderson"—for two full pages. (Henry Anderson).

*****

"I don't see how anybody can have their progress charts or whatever they are, just a minute there, I mean those three white charts on the closet doors, completed. I suppose it could be done if you have the ambition, physically and mentally. Believe me, I'm trying sort of hard not to write a bunch of senseless sentences, because that gets to be a super drag. One thing which is really strange is having to write two pages of anything and its seems at time sooo difficult, like right now. Also I have seven and a quarter pages to do of that two page crap, so I guess I'll have to start writing anything just so I get a good grade. Oh, oh, its starting already. I guess I'll have to write a bunch of crap but I don't like to do that.

 I wish I could fly. I don't see how anybody can stay at an altitude 40 feet below zero which is closest to one zerox or xerox sulk sulk ha ha astronauts coina phrase breaking into the center ho ha I wish I had done this when I had spare time instead of wasting my precious time then I wouldn't have to make up all the assignments. All F's is becoming a reality. I suppose I'll fight a little probably just enough to pass by the hair on my fingernail. None shall be that which is not here for I shall cause the worlds collision which can be proven just beyond belief. That I exist among others a belief that shall not be proven. Through eternities ants rule. The world you can mother a collision of minds and explore the inner galaxies but I suppose two pages is more and I read and summerize ahah what a farce. (Joe Fork).

*****

"I am written two pages I am written two pages I am written two pages I am written two pages"---for two pages. (Clayton).

*****

4. Assignment: "Mr. Aston"

The reason for this assignment was twofold. One, I wanted to know what the students thought of me as a teacher. Secondly, I was interested in their conception of a life style outside of their immediate experience.

Assignment for Today.
Write a biography of me. How long have I been teaching? What other jobs have I had? Do I have a family? What sort of place do I live in? What are my likes and dislikes? Is there anything you like, or dislike, about me? Use what information you may have and make up the rest. You do not have to sign your papers.

"I want to skip all the other crap on the board except for: "What you think about me." I think that your approaching teaching all wrong. You should have done this before. Now we hate you and I don't think you can change it. One good point, you throw good parties."
(Suzi Mantele)

*****

"Richard J. Aston was born in England. When he was young he went to boarding school. I think he skipped a lot of grades and became a jockey. When he was old enough I think he travelled around the world and, when he was in China, he married a Chinese girl. Then he came to America and went to some university.

I think he lives in San Francisco now in a little apartment with painted windows, a lot of posters, no furniture — just pillows on the floor, and a whole lot of books.

I think at first when he came to America he had some small job to support himself. Before he moved to San Francisco he studied drama and went to Hollywood and got in some T.V. series. He watches T.V. a couple of times a week. When he does I think he watches suspense movies — things like the late, late show. His favorite foods are foreign and real delicacy things. Your wife has long hair and doesn't wear much make-up. You think she is very beautiful. You sit around at night with her on the pillows, with candles burning, drinking wine and eating potato chips and kissing her." (Valerie Valias).

*****

"Mr. Aston sir, I think you are one of the (if not the) meanest teachers in the school. You are one of few teachers in this school I really hate. I am being very serious and I am not kidding around with you. You always crack down on me harder than you do the other kids in the class who fool around. This I do not dig very much. If I had much choice, I would get the heck out this class. Ever since Mr. Edwards has gone, it has not been the same in here.

I do not want to make any guesses about your personal life. I really don't think it's any of my business. I do not wish to say any thing about myself or else you will no doubt know what on. If you figure out who I am, please do not crack down on me any harder than you have." (Harry Bippo).

*****

"There was once a large fancy zoo in the southwestern part of England. Well, in this zoo there were six gorillas. One day the zoo keeper noticed something strange in the gorilla cage and, as he opened the cage door, one gorilla slipped out. At once the zoo keeper sent out an all-points bulletin for the capture of the escaped gorilla.

Well, this gorilla didn't have anything to do so he slipped on board a ship that was going to China. Finally, after many days of sailing, the boat landed in China. Walking down the streets of China with nothing to do he suddenly grabbed a girl that he thought was pretty and got her on a boat to San Francisco.

When they arrived in San Francisco the gorilla found that everyone thought he was ugly so he went into a store and bought a human costume. The gorilla put the mask and costume on, which fit perfectly except for the top of his head and a part of his chin.

Then he went to a place to get married and married the girl that he grabbed in China.

Then feeling very bored, he went to see about a job. First he worked as a paper boy and a few odd jobs like that. Then he went to see about a longshoreman's job, and a place to live (his wife was tired of living in a cave). After being a longshoreman for a while he went to Sausalito (across the Golden Gate Bridge) to see about being a teacher. He was accepted almost immediately.

So here he works as a teacher, which is really pretty easy because all he has to do is sit in his chair and make the kids write pages for him to read. But he is still afraid that someone may discover his true identity because of his gorilla-like habits." (Wildflower Weed).

*****

"I can't make up things about you. All I know is your name is Mr. Aston and I know what you look like. You have been teaching for four years. If I make something about you may take it the wrong way and think I'm an ass, which I am, but you might think of me as more than an ass, which I'm not. What is the purpose of this? Anyway I wanna read. (Karen).

*****

"I don't like you. I don't care if you live or die because you are a fucking bitch and a lying asshole. You don't have a wife because what lady would like to live with you? I think you like fried ants, your favorite movie star is Bette Davis and your hobby is looking for dead bodies." (Georgie).

*****

"You live within yourself and seem to belong in another place because you travel. Your interests are in foreign places and different cultures. You don't have a family, maybe a dog. The schools you have been to have been very different from each other. The jobs you have had were probably in the Peace Corps or something to do with foreign people. You like to work with people.

You are not married. You are in your mid-thirties and like un-American food." (Vouix).

*****

"You live in a very high society place with people who are prejudiced and snotty. I think you have a long ugly face, sort of Scottish terrier with long ugly hair on his face. You have no family. Your hobbies are teaching law, Play-boy bunnies, the beach and girls. You've been to private schools. Your other jobs have been desk jobs with a pretty, snotty secretary. You look like you are about thirty. Your favorite food is shish-kebab." (Love Bug).

*****

"Mr. Aston is a mean punk. He don't take no stuff. He can be a good teacher if he wants to be. Mr. Aston don't like some students because some students don't like him. He like all the smart people because they understand what he talks about. The dumb people don't understand what he talks about. He could make the dumb people understand but he doesn't want to." (Hal).

*****

"Mr. Aston grew up in England and was born in the year 1869 and today is one hundred years old. Now he has a beard and a few specks of gray hair except he dyed it, but the dye is wearing off and he can't do anything about it. Every day he wears a tie, everyday he wears hip-huggers and he doesn't wear glasses.

When he was twenty he went out and got a job as a movie star but every movie he was in he had to be Frankenstein or some other kind of monster. He didn't like this job so he quit and started to travel around the world. He stopped when he got to England and married this fat, monster-looking woman and settled down in a big house with six rooms, no kids, six birds, two dogs, four cats and a rabbit and I don't like you." (Jake Smoot).

*****

"Mr. Aston is fifty and hitting it hard. He lives in some old house with one bed and nothing else. His wife is not black because no black woman would want him. He's got a white wife and her hair is as long as my baby finger. He looks like hot chilipeppers and is the ugliest person I ever have seen." (Penny).

*****

"I think you are the ugliest man I have ever seen, and I have seen a lot of people. But you beat them all. Your wife can not put up with you as you seem like the type to nag your wife all the time and she is going to pieces. You act like she is going to leave you. You act like you have bad trouble and when you come to school you take it out on us. When you have a problem you should stop doing us like that or we will jump on you." (McKibben).

*****

"I believe that Mr. Aston is an Englishman and he would be willing to fight the revolution over again. He probably lives in a place that looks like him-- not too clean, not too dirty--just about average. He doesn't have a wide wardrobe — about five pairs of bell-bottoms, seven shirts and two suits. He probably lives in San Francisco, San Rafael or Tiburon. He looks like he about thirty-six. He looks like the kind of man who would run away from home or desert his family because he cannot support them. I can tell he isn't married because of his clothes. If he was married he would dress better." (Pimpy).

*****

"I don't like you at all. Most teachers and grown-ups I don't like. I have my reasons why and it is no concern of anybody else. That is all I want to write and I don't want to have any conferences." (Kat Hart)

*****

"I don't like you at all. Really, there's nothing I like about you. You are the kind of man who can't take what you dish out. Who would want to know what your wife looks like, maybe some other people care but I don't. For all I know your wife could look like a witch. For one thing, I don't like the way you teach. When somebody is trying to work you turn out the lights. You just try to make people hate you and you know it just as well as I do. Maybe you don't like me but I don't like you either. Maybe you think we should get on our knees and beg your friendship. All you do is look for trouble. You think you are really something but you ain't shit." (Henry).

*****

"I know you is prejudiced. I hate a prejudiced bitch like you. You don't have a wife because no bitch can like a bitch. You are fucked-up in the face and your pants sag on your ass." (Franklin).

*****

"Well, come to think of it I think you live in a hippie house. I don't really care what goes on about your family or pets. I don't know what kind of jobs you've had and don't care." (Laverta Jean).

*****

"He wears odd ties but he isn't that bad because when somebody does good work he buys them ice cream. He looks like he might like pets. He taught in Chinese schools. He probably lived in China. Some of your jobs might have been raking leaves or cutting grass. He might like shows like the Mr. Ed show or Gilligan's Island or Gomer Pyle. I think you are about thirty-one and your favorite food is squid salad and Chinese rice." (Anon).

****

5. Class Rules for Students

In an attempt to reduce some structure to the class, I attempted to implement some rules.

Response

```
            CLASS RULES FOR STUDENTS

               ROOM 2, MR. ASTON


You will talk in class only when called upon by the
teacher.  If you wish to say something raise your hand.

You will stay in your seat throughout the period unless
given permission to get up.

You will not eat in class.

You will be required to turn in at least one written
assignment per week.

You are required to complete at least one reading
assignment per week.

At least once a week you will have an individual
conference with the teacher to discuss your progress
and to enable you to voice suggestions and complaints.

The teacher will be available for conference during
announced class time, from 8am to 8:30am, during recess
and lunch, and from 2:45 to 4:30pm.



I have read and understand the above rules.




                                _____
                                    (Student's signature)
```

Emy

Signed under protest

"Mr. Aston has cancelled the rights of freedom of speech and the freedom of assembly. The following people would like to have that changed." Signed: Thirty students, with the added comments:

*****

"Mr. Aston, in the class you got some shitty assed rules. You can't get out of your seat for water, and you can not talk in class. You said to write about you but we don't know nothing about you." (Clayton).

*****

"He came to Martin Luther King not knowing anything about it but what he had read about it in the papers and what other people say. He got there knowing nothing or nobody in the class. He didn't know about how they acted. So, he made up strict rules. He wanted to see how they reacted to his rules. They petitioned and tried everything in the book to get rid of him but they did not succeed. Now that he said we tried to get rid of him in the democratic way. To some people he is changing but others do not want to accept it. They look at him as a Mr. Aston of the past. He is trying to be nice but they won't let him." (Tony).

****

6. Teachers
Assignment: What do you think about your teachers at MLK?

"I is going to write about a certain teacher whom is bugging me. I am going to refer to this teacher as "it". It starts in the morning with a fake smile and a "thank you", for what I never know. It then proceeds to name off a list five feet long of assignments to be done in fifteen minutes. When it is done it proceeds to yell at someone, stops, say thank you, smiles, and yells at someone else. Then it says shut up and proceeds to talk for the rest of the period. At a fire alarm it marches out and lines the class up. It yells at a body ten feet above it, oh, I wouldn't want to be it's wife or husband. It makes you stand up in front of a class and recite the paper you wrote. You have to sweat, turn red, get sick, shake and fall all over. Are you nervous? Maybe your voice goes down when you read or talk to the class." (Vouix).

*****

"The teacher is boring. She also makes me sick. I would rather listen to you talk to us about pissing in the pure cane sugar from Hawaii when you were a longshoreman and of people falling into sausage making machines. I wonder what goes into Cambell's vegetable and beef soup.

She's sooooo boring I'm on the verge of sleep. Yawn. How do these poor little kids stand it? Jees Christ don't she ever shut up. Look around the class. Everybody is bored assless. I'm almost too tired to write. I haven't heard a word she said. I was reading cigarette ads I was so bored. Shit, she even had the speech written before she said it. Wonder who wrote it? Spiro Agnew?" (Adam).

*****

"Roses are red,
Violets are blue.
We don't learn anything
From teachers like you.

No offense son."
(Fritz the Cat)

*****

"Mrs. Hinton is a very nice teacher sometimes when we are nice to her and we do our work. I think she is very nice cause she lets you go to the bathroom and music class and some of the teachers don't let you do that cause they thinks you are missing out in their class to go to music. Mrs. Hinton is a very cool teacher and I like her more than any of my other teachers.

Mr. Drake is not cool one bit to me cause all he does is just yell at us for the hell of it and I don't think it is cool one bit to me. I know one thing; if he should say one thing to me I am going to cuss him right back out. That is why I hate him.

I like Mr. Gill very much cause I am learning a lot in his class. He is a very cool teacher to me. I enjoy being in all his classes.

I don't like Mr. Aston at all cause he is getting like Mr. Drake and I don't dig on that one bit. Mr. Aston is always making us sit in the class and just write all the time and I don't dig on that at all."
(Francis).

*****

"Mrs. Hinton, if you don't already know, is a bitch. She tells everyone to do an assignment and then talks for an hour after that. Today she moved me to the front of the class because I talk with Malcolm too much. She told us to do an assignment and then went on talking. I told her to be quiet and then shut up. She said O.K. and promptly went to her desk and told Malcolm to be quiet because Karen wants you to. (Malcolm's desk is right near hers.) Also, she didn't pick on him in particular, just because he was mumbling. I said, "Mrs. Hinton, I was talking about you, not anyone else." But she didn't hear me.

I'm going to have to write on the back of this paper because Mrs. Hinton is skimpy on paper and she won't let me have two papers.

I was at the school board meeting on Monday night and when I heard you were going to have to go it made me mad because you are the best teacher we have. Mae Wellman also is one of the best teachers is leaving too. All of the other teachers like Thomas and Dowd are bad teachers and they are the ones who should be going.

Your class has been the best of all of them so far this year and it is a real drag that they are taking you away from the school. Mae should also stay because she also relates to the kids just like you do. It just seems funny to me that all the teachers who relate to the students are not going to be around next year. What this school needs the most is good teachers who can relate to the students.

Ian and I think you are one of the best teachers in this school except sometimes when you are mad at someone and you take it out on everyone. You seem to be the opposite of Mrs. Hinton, that's why I like you. Hinton plays too many games. She's as plastic as hell and such a bitch I always dread coming into her class. Maybe if you taught her subject I might not like you either. But I'm sure I wouldn't dread it half as much if you taught it instead of that bitch." (Joe Fork)

*****

"Today in the math class the teacher made me move because someone was bothering me. This little incident has stirred up all that old hate. I t has sprouted the seed. The hate is growing. I need to devise some way in which I can get back at that dammed teacher. Who chopped down the cherry tree? Oh yes. It was George Washington. That was what happened to my hate. The tree was chopped down but there is still a sprout in the stump. A tiny sprout is still able to grow into a large tree." (Mark).

*****

"Nick Names
Mr. Aston--flapjack, snoopy or aspirin (because you give us a headache).
Mrs. Larson--bald eagle.
Mr. Bearsh—hairy.
Mr. Pockrus--pack rat.
Mr. Flynn--ball head.

Mr. Flores--sweet pea or Herman, Herman.
Mr. Sidhu--ich boo.
Mr. Tolliver [vice-principal] — Uncle Tom.
Mr. Walton {principal} — Sidney." (Boxhead)

*****

"The substitute for Mr. Drake is really freaky. She must read the *Independent Journal* a lot. She doesn't realize we are in the eighth grade. When she was talking about the starving childen she gave us a very interesting fact (uh huh) and I quote, "Do you realize that actually in this United States, a wealthy country (suspense building every minute), that there are actually people starving?" Gee, no shit, but now that we know that what can be done?" (Xathier X. Zeus)

*****

"Some of my teachers make me sick and some I really like. I am not going to mention any names because that is for me to know and you to find out. Most of my classes are boring and the person that is supposed to be teaching the class does not handle it very well and I will be glad to get away from here so I won't have to look at their face again. Anyway if your so-called teacher would act their own age maybe I can learn a little more." (Puddingtang).

****

7. Thoughts While in Class

These free-flowing thoughts, written while in class, I found particularly intriguing--perhaps because they recalled memories of my school years

———————

"Back to classroom activities.... The discussion has already been diverted by many multi-colored basket balls with sea- gull wings floating discreetly through the classroom air along with a yellow and purple pair of knickerbockers being shoved along ignorantly by an epsilon minus semi-moron mole who really doesn't know what an ass he's making of himself." (Bippo).

*****

"This is so boring it is absolutely killing me. Why must we go through unbearable torture? So blah. The teacher is a rat and I must scribble or I shall fall to pieces. Why? Why? Why? Oh dear, I will scream if the rat doesn't shut up. New York, New York, doesn't especially love this study either. She must scribble on her paper to keep together also. Too many minutes will come before the bell rings..

That bell gets on my nerves, especially in the morning when it interrupts your nerves. Uhhhhhhh! Paper and chalk. I do hate them except if the paper has no lines on it. But then, what rat would be courteous enough to give us that?

I wonder, not white paper, no other, because I have been seeing white paper every day since first grade. Enough to make you sick. Enough to get sick. Want to cut. Can't. Too bad.

In the fourth grade you had to make perfect numbers and letters. I absolutely despise anything like that now. Especially when they are lined up on the board for you to see. People think they are beautiful. They are tremendously ugly. People want to write like that? No imagination. Like ticky-tacky houses lined up with flat lawns for status. Can't let the neighbors see if you step on it. Bad for the reputation. Sickening, kids gigle, talk quietly, write letters. Along comes a rat. No, no, no. Can't communicate.

Must crack up instead and listen. Listen to gibberish nonsense that you do not understand. Don't understand. Don't listen. Don't listen. Communicate again. Want to cuss the rat out, but no. Can't communicate. Regimented. So awful and stuffy. Must learn other things. Can't stand lectured nonsense. Makes no sense so no one listens. No one learns and the kids get blamed. So terrible in this box." (Vouix)

*****

"The Kick. It all happened this morning. I came to school and went to my first period class. I sat down in the front of the row. Then as soon as I sat down this nut crazy fool named Shirley, this fool, just turned around and kicked me. "Ouch!"

This fool kicked me and made me bleed so I called to Mr. Aston, "This fool kicked me and made me bleed." Who kicked you Dude?" "Shirley did. Can't you hear? I told you at least ten times already." "Shirley, you kick Dude one more time and you will go home." (Dude).

*****

"How come that weird, tall man with the slowly growing baldspot keeps looking at me and smiling. Could he suspect? Is he a faggot? Is he trying to scare me? How come he doesn't do anything? Like the song-
"*And you know something is happening here, but you don't know what it is.*"

I want to fill this page in because I don't like to turn in half a page and it doesn't look good. Even though my thoughts are wandering the mountie must get his man and I must complete this page in spite of my hopeless condition of thought-wanderfullness. Well here we go, we've almost made it. Yahoooo!

It's Wednesday and third period with group K at Martin Luther King School. Mr. Aston is walking around making me nervous. Joan Baez is singing "Love is Just a Four-Letter Word." The studious students have their heads bent studiously over their studies. Mr. Aston is still walking around. I wonder if he's in a bad mood. He smiles when you least expect it. I wonder if that means he's feeling good or bad. He just came up to me and said, "You don't want me to bother you again?" I said, "Hi." Then he went away. But he was smiling the whole time. I don't know why.

Now he's over by his desk thumbing through the papers we just finished. He's smiling. Bob Dylan is singing "Mr. Tambourine Man." I feel comfortable right now. There's the usual moderate noise in the class. Now he looks irritated. He is.

Since I just wrote "He is" I've been waiting a few minutes. Now he looks fine. I think he's in a good mood now but he hasn't smiled yet. He just smiled. He's reading someone's paper and smiling.

He just finished drinking his coffee and asked me if I wasn't sure I wanted to do a. study of Oriental literature. I think I might. He seems like he's in a really good mood. He's going through all these books now.

Whenever I think of Mr. Aston I think of books and records. No, not really. At least, not all of the time. Mr. Aston just showed me two books to read but I had already read them.

Well, its almost time to go and I haven't filled up these two pages yet. I don't want to read *Our Language Today*. I'd rather write because my teeth hurt and I feel lousy and I'm scaired. I look at a picture of heaven, hell and the garden of delights .

 Plunging through three dimensional checker boards in thick layers, each checker contains a little fantasy to watch. A green light swirls. I try to make it stand still and force myself through it. It turns paler and gets bigger and at the last minute my attention drifts and it disappears.
I can't see, I can't stand, I can't reason
I can lie
I don't know when to stop." (Adam).

*****

"There was this classroom it had about twenty young men and young women, and it was a very strict teacher, his name is Mr. Aston.

One day Mr. Aston was in a bad mood so he decided that he was going to take it out on his pupils. So when the students came in and sat down the teacher began to yell right away. He said that he had gave us an assignment and he wanted to know why we didn't have it. Some of the people told Mr. Aston that they had it in their desk and he yelled at them.

As soon as Mr. Aston got finished yelling a guest came in and Mr. Aston got really nice to everybody. He put up his front. He pretended to be so nice and everything that everybody sit there with their mouth open and couldn't say a word.

Like I told you once before I enjoy the class the way you did have it. Now I can't say that anymore. I just hate thinking about going to school in the morning because I know that I have to come to social science." (Tamila Shalon).

*****

"In 1492, Columbus sailed the ocean blue, on August 3rd Leif Erickson came first. Red sky at morning sailor take warning. Red sky at night, sailor's delight. "Thank you Erickson you're a good man." I can write, says Leif Erickson, about me. "Sidhu, Sidhu, scooly-do," says McKibben. "The telephone is on the line, how poetic," says Harold.

"Plane figure is anything that can be a closed figure," says Sidhu merrily to the class. He gives a menacing look to Wildflower Weed about writing in class. "The most polygon," says Sidhu. "Jake, Jake," says Sidhu to Jake about Jake talking. Edward gives word to class about visitors from out of town in class. Slight mumble from among naughty boys in class. "You will get sufficient time to write down." says Sidhu to a few disinterested students.

I have just got a warning from Sidhu about writing in this class. "Jake, you are not attending," says Sidhu. Love Bug enters with knitting in hand. Mao says Sidhu doesn't know what he's talking about. Leif Erickson disagrees. "Wartex of de ray is da letta. A," says Sidhu. Sidhu arguing with Little Green Man and Ella about leaving class.

My thanks to all my classmates in helping me write about this. Bye-bye. "Yes, Sidhu, I am attending to you." "Burp." (Harry Bippo).

*****

"I am hot, tired and dirty right now. Plus very thirsty. The drinking water is hot. I am now in our sailing class (a special activity on Friday afternoons) at Martin Luther King School. I have just heard something. It seems that Mr. Walton, Mr. Simmons and you are absent. The class was just told to do anything they want to down on the grass. I wanted very much to learn something about sailing today.

As I was saying there is a rumor going around that you, Mr. Walton and Mr. Simmons might be together right now. It is a nice day, hot but cool so I won't get mad if what I am thinking is true. The rumor is that you, Mr. Walton and Mr. Simmons are out sailing today. There is not much wind so I hope you are not sailing. But so help me, if you guys are on a sailing boat, drinking beer and eating sandwiches you have had it!!! Wait. I have just seen Mr. Walton. Well, he got out of that fast. So its just the two of you. Good for Mr. Walton. He is going to give us a lesson in our class. I hope it is a good one. And if you are out sailing today I do hope that you have a very good time." (Roberts).

*****

"There is a camera that the teacher is pointing at people and pulling the trigger. Don't point that thing at me. I feel like I'm being hunted. Everyone is laughing and having fun and I feel like I'm snarling inside. When that camera was first pointed at me I felt like a cornered animal. I don't know why. Its not as bad as all that. I guess yes it is. Worse." (Washington Irving).

*****

"Cats out. Cats out. Dogs in. Dogs in. Look out. Look out. Don't. Don't. Let let, the the cat in, cat in. Cause dogs in, dogs in. Fish jumped. Fish jumped. Out out. Look out. Look out. Don't. Don't. Let the let the cat cat in in. Cause fish jumped fish jumped out out. Birds out. Birds out. Flew out. Flew out, of cage of cage. Look out. Look out. Don't let don't let. Cat in, cat in. Cause birds out, birds out. Rats out. Rat out. Look out. Look out. Don't. Don't let let cat in cat in. Rats out. Rats out. Chicks out. Chicks out. Look out. Look out. Chicks out. Chicks out. Don't. Don't Let let cat in. Chicks out. Chicks out.

Songs out. Songs out. Look out, look out. Songs out. Songs out. Look out, look out. Close close. Your your mouth. Songs out. Songs out. Don't play. No fun, no fun. No use, no use. Look out, look out. Stop, stop. Don't, don't. No music, no music.

Hurts, hurts, my ears ears. Look out, look out. Stop, stop. Don't, don't. Stop, stop. Don't look, don't look. Bad, bad for your eyes. No good, no good." (Wildflower Weed).

*****

"I have to think about math. Shit. I hope the coffee see me through. Oh shit. People are getting in the test tube fucking. It scares me. I'm not ready for math. $Y+6-6=Y=22$. I used to have nightmares about shit like this. Forty-two over Y plus five equals a pile of shit. People swear to release tension..
Godamnsonofamotherfuckingcock- suckingshiteatingbitch.
I don't feel any better. Once I saw a very greasy gasoline man with a button that said, "I feel fine, feel me." It made me sick. Pretty little girls never wear shit like that. Oh shit, the math test." (Adam).

*****

"Outline of the Bull We Got Fed. We had a little old, pro-Vietnam, Sarge give us a bunch of junk about statistics and about how honest old Nixon is. How anybody could get brainwashed by the U.S. Army so effectively is beyond me. We tried to ask him about Cambodia and Laos and I would have asked him about Mei-Lai and "taking orders from commanding officers," "It's in the enlistment papers, you know," had not Mrs. Larson butted in, saying, "Thank you for coming, Sgt. Connelly." You said to write what he said. Well, he didn't tell me anything except how good the army was and also how to blow your young life out the window by making it a career." (Harry Bippo).

*****

"This army dude talked about many things but I did not pay any attention because I am not interested in the armed services or any of these things. I didn't listen to his speech." (Mark).

*****

"The talk that the man was giving was very boring. I really wasn't interested in what he had to say so I went to sleep and didn't pay attention to him." (Little Green Man).

*****

"Today we talked about many different things. I think it is good class if some of the people would stop jive a round so much. They were asking silly questions about is hamburger better than pussy. And they were to asking Mr. Aston do he get a lot of pussy. The ones that ask these silly things are Johnny, Georgie and Randy but Mr. Aston said that he was going to get them out of the class. When a person do ask a good question they always say, "You think you know so much." (Bettina).

*****

"Big, beige, and metal. Four wide, three tall, slanted at the top. Silver handles, round lock, serial numbered. Three vents, three vents. Empty all. Screw it! I don't want to describe a fucking locker. I got better things to do than sit around on my blue grained ass and write about some lousey lockers.

Rafferty is going around checking on them to find "dope" if they could, and some times they can, but not me. They ain't gonna catch ole Adam, no they ain't. Not me, I'm too slick. I'll stash it real cool, yeseree they won't catch me. I'll run fast an hard and eat it all." (Adam).

8. Assignment: What books have you read?

Before I went to MLK I was under the impression that teenagers did not read much and that T.V. and movies had replaced books. More importantly, I had been told that many young people could hardly read at all.

This seemed to be borne out when, on my second day in class, I called the students, one by one, up to my desk to read aloud from the textbook. Many stumbled over every word, and the class as a whole seemed in pretty bad shape. But, as one boy, who had read very poorly, walked away from the desk I saw a book in his back pocket. It was *To Kill a Mockingbird*. Something didn't jibe. If he can't read — why the book?

Subsequently I saw many "non-readers" engrossed in the sports section of the newspaper. It appeared that many of the kids actually did a lot of reading, provided the books had nothing to do with school. In fact, it seemed that some were illiterate only in the matter of reading textbooks. Due either to lack of interest, or motivation, or tension, the words became indecipherable when they were asked to read. When finally, I asked the kids to list the books they had read I was greatly surprised at the extent of the list and the level of maturity of many of the books.

The list below has been greatly edited, as I eliminated most of the common children's books that were mentioned in order to emphasize the upper levels of interest.

"This is a pretty dumb thing to ask people to do cause they can't remember all the books they've read. Nobody can remember that." (Elsa).

*****

The Combined List

Adventures in the Skin Trade
All the Things You Ever Wanted to Know About Sex
Animal Farm
The American Way of Death
Another Country
Autobiography of Lincoln Steffens
Autobiography of Malcolm X
Basics of Digital Computers
Becket
The Bending Cross
The Big Strike
Big Time Buck White
The Biography of Sidney Poitier
Black Bondage
Black Boy
The Black Curriculum
Black is Beautiful
Black Like Me
Black on White
Black Power
Black Pow-wow
Black Rage
Blackboard Jungle
Bob Dylan
Brave New World
Bread and Wine
Bus Stop
Call it Sleep
Candy
Cannery Row
Catch 22
Catcher in the Rye
Chapman Report
Charlie in the Chocolate Factory
Childhood's End
Children Who Stayed Alone
Communitas
Confederate General from Big Sur
The Cool World
Dandelion Wine
David and Lisa
Dead End School
Death be not Proud
Diary of Anne Frank
Dibs in Search of Self
Do It
Doctor Strangelove
Down Main Street
Drug Abuse
Drug Book
The Drug Experience
Drugs and the Mind
The Dubliners
Earth House Hold
The Ecstasy Drugs
Edgar Cayce on Religion and Psychic Experience
Education and Ecstasy

Elephant Lust
The Eyes of Reason
Exploring the Psychic World
Fahrenheit 451
Fellowship of the Ring
Giovanni's Room
The Girl Who Loved Black
Go Tell it on the Mountain
Gods, Graves and Scholars
Gone with the Wind
The Good Earth
Goodbye Columbus
The Graduate
The Grapes of Wrath
Grass Pipe
Greek Philosophy
To Have and Have Not
The Heart is a Lonely Hunter
Hell's Angels
Hiroshima
Hot Rocks
Human Comedy
The Hungry Husband
I Robot
Illustrated Man
In Dubious Battle
In Watermelon Sugar
Inner City Mother Goose
It Can't Happen Here
Jazz Country
L.S.D.
Lady Chatterley's Lover
Langston Hughes Poetry
The Learning Tree

Leopold and Loeb
Letting Go
Life of a Prostitute
Lilies of the Field
The Long Summer
Look Homeward Angel
Look Out Whitey Black Power Gonna Get Your Mamma
Lord of the Flies
Love and Sex in Plain Language
The Love Everybody Crusade
Love in a Dark House
The Love Machine
Love, Sex and Racism in America
Machines of Joy
The Magic Christian
Malcolm X Speaks
Man-child in the Promised Land
Marihuana Papers
Martian Chronicles
Mash Up
The Me Nobody Knows
Medicine for Melancholy
The Medium is the Massage
Member of the Wedding
Midsummer's Night Dream
Miracle Drugs
Moveable Feast
The Naked Ape
Native Son

The Need to be Loved
The Neighbors are Scaring My Wolf
Never Trust a Naked Bus Driver
Nigger
Nigger Bible
Nights of Love and Laughter
The Night Visitor
1984
No Bed of Roses
Of Mice and Men
Old Man and the Sea
On Being Negro in America
On Shooting an Elephant
On the Drumhead
The Outsiders
Patch of Blue
A Pictorial History of the Negro
Pimp
Poetry of the Negro
Poor Cow
The Private World of Pablo Picasso
Professional Thief
Quotations from Chairman Mao Tse-tung
A Raisin in the Sun
Reminiscences of the Cuban Revolutionary War
Revolt on Alpha C
Rivers of Blood, Years of Darkness
Rosemary's Baby
Schvambrantra
The Secret Language
See How They Come
Sex and the Adolescent
Sex and the Single Girl
Snow Country
Some Faces in the Crowd
Soul Brother and Sister Lou
Soul on Ice
Steppenwolf
The Stranger
Stranger in a Strange Land
The Story of Christine Jorgensen
The Story of Medgar Evers
The Struggle Within
Tales of a Troubled Land
Teaching as a Subversive Activity
This Stranger, My Son
This Train is Bound for Glory
Thousand Cranes
To Kill a Mockingbird
To Sir with Love
Tortilla Flat
Trout Fishing in America
Twenty-six Ways of Looking at a Black Man
Uncle Tom's Children
The Unsatisfactory Male
Up the Down Staircases
The Valachi Papers
Valley of the Dolls

The View From the Back of the Bus	White Boy
Walden Pond	Woodstock
The Way Its Spozed to Be	Yes I Can
We Have Always Lived in the Castle	Z
Weep Not Child	Zap Comics

*****

"I'm asleep. How do you expect me to write when I'm asleep? I should shut up. I don't think I can remember all the books I've read. How can I list all the books if I can't remember them? Huh? Answer me that. Well? Come on. Huh? You can't answer. I think the list of books you want us to write is some type of busy work. Actually, I can't tell what it is for. If it was a list of class library books I could understand it." (Washington Irving).

*****

"Mr. Aston, I refuse to write down any more books because I am sick of this and am using up all the paper. What are you trying to do to me? Ruin me for life and turn me against reading? Well you made me get a big headache and stay up too late. I will not tell you any more books I have read. I am reading about five on and off now but can't write their names down because I am sick of books!" (Vouix).

****

9. Assignment: Textbooks

Many of you have complained that textbooks are "uninteresting," "biased, and "tell lies." What do you think?

───────────

"Well I think that the books give us a lot of information. I also think that the school books do not always tell the truth because they are humans and human aren't always perfect. Everybody makes mistakes." (Pamela Marie).

*****

"I have been using textbooks for nine years. They have never helped me. Some have slowed me down.

I didn't read well and almost never did until third grade when I started reading mystery stories.

I believe this was because of the textbooks from which they taught us to read. Everything I've ever read and "learned" from a textbook has either slowed me down, been forgotten, or learned much better from some place else.

There is nothing more untrue (that I can think of, besides a politician) than a textbook. Controversial subjects are either banned or controlled. When I was in fifth grade the students, the teacher and the two student teachers, looked for a British side of the war.

We couldn't find one. The Revolutionary War is pretty uncontroversial now, but you still can't find the British side. In Russia the Communists finally decided that Stalin was bad.

You can only find his name in two places in *Land of the Free*. In *Civics in Action*, [the two required text] there are only Two, <u>two</u>, sentences on the Korean War are mentioned, but no mention of all the blood that was spilt to stop communism.

Civics in Action was printed in 1967 and, in the same sentence as Korea, Vietnam was mentioned with no mention of the genocide of an entire people.

Land of the Free is a little more truthful about Vietnam but it states that "communists" had taken over North Vietnam and started to move into the South. There was no mention of which communists or that we were asked to enter Vietnam by anyone.

In both books communism is not mentioned at all as a good thing or even just a power but always as an evil dictatorship.

In mentioning Cuba (in *Land of the Free*) there is nothing about the exploitation of a people, only that it is run by a "dictator". It acts as if the United States stopped Russia from continuing to arm Cuba.

Textbooks are all full of shit but some have more shit than others." (Adam).

*****

"Do school books tell lies?

True!!! School books do tell lies. They are always telling how free and better this country is than any other country.

When this country has ghettos and people are being suppressed how can they say that when it is not true.

In this country we have racist people who hate black, red, yellow and brown because of the color of the skin. How can those books say this is a better country?

It really makes me mad these books can say how good this country is and its not true at all. Because in my opinion this country is a racist, fascist, greedy country." (Ian).

*****

"Well, I do not know if school books tell lies, but I do not like to read white people's books that they make for school.

One thing, I was not living in the olden days when they had the Civil War and other things. If I was living in those days I would know.

And another thing, why don't they have blacks in books? I know they did something in wars." (Penny).

*****

"*Land of the Free* says this is a free country. It also says it is better than any other country. Almost everything they say is slanted.

The idea of this system is to keep this system in power. It doesn't matter who controls it.

I think the books get away with a lot of bull. They don't mention Thomas Paine who was, in my opinion, more important than George Washington, either now or in the 18th century.

If this is what history really is like maybe we should have stayed with England. If we get taught out of these books, thank you, I'll stay ignorant.

Actually, Tom Paine has half a paragraph in *Land of the Free* which doesn't say a dammed thing. The book says parliament was taxing the colonists and they didn't like it so they revolted." (Washington Irving)

*****

"Do school books tell lies? Yes. The books tell us that this country is great and beautiful and perfect and that the Soviet Union is ugly and mean and horrible.

They tell us that communism is horrible and unfair and wrong and that capitalism is nice and fair and right.

They say white is superior and that black is inferior.

They say the Indians horribly massacred innocent people and that we stopped their horrid ways and gave them land." (Simon).

****

10. Assignment: "Yesterday...."

"Last night was far out. There was some beautiful lightning. It flashed across the sky around my house. It was blue, white, purple and red. You could see it in San Francisco and K.M.P.X. was playing a long raga by a La Rocca King.

People were in the clouds shooting up on lightning some of it spilled out of their spikes so we could see it. Other cloud people and angels were drinking distilled rain water and smoking cloud plants. There's alcohol in clouds that doesn't come down with the rain. In storms they have parties. Only the bad ones shoot lightning. Some sniff. All this only happens at parties." (Adam).

*****

"It is a cold day in winter but the sun is shining. The ground is muddy from recent rains and the creek is high. I feel that the time is good to take out my kayak to test my skills. So, I gather all the necessary equipment that is needed and carry it down to the creek. I pull on the tight spray cover, fasten the seat in the boat and fasten the spray cover to the rim of the cockpit.

It is a hard pull up the fast current and I need to rest often. I finally get to the slower, deeper part of the creek where padding is easier. It is easy enough to be easy but has a faint trace of hardness. I gradually course into brisker current. There are many eddies where there are dips in the bank. I turn into one to rest.

After resting I turn out of it as though I was completely unaware of the strong current there. I teeter alarmingly slow about 60° to one side and then 180° in the other. I panic! I feel that I will drown. I need to get away from this tight-fitting spray cover. Gradually I over come this panic. I need only to think enough to pull the spray cover off the rim of the cockpit. I do and am released out last.

I swim nearly to shore and empty out my kayak. I chase after my paddles that have gone downstream at an amazingly fast speed and catch them at last. Then I run back to my boat, get in and go home.

I feel that this was educational to me because I learned many, many things. I learned that a kayaker needs to be careful coming out of an eddie and to lean downstream. I also learned to brace with my paddle when coming out of an eddie.

I also learned things that could be attached to other times, out of the kayak. They are, to think ahead, and not to panic. If I had thought ahead I would have realized that I would tip over, and if I hadn't stopped panicking I would have surely drowned." (Mark).

*****

"Well, one day I was talking to Henry over by the pond an' I says to him I says, "You!, ain't no fishing allowed here", an he says to me, "Fuck the sign, aan'th' law I'll fish when I feel like it." Well I says, "Well right on then," I says, an' he pulled out a lot a fishing line an' kick in a rotting ol' log an' pulled out a bag an' a small bottle of Gallo Port an' I pulled out a pack of papers and we smoked weed and drank cheep shit and got stoned. Then we fished." (Adam).

*****

"Last night our door bell rang, and we said come in, but no one came. So I went to the .door and two white men where standing there and they where all wet and dirty and they ask us if they could use our telephone, and I screamed and slammed the door and ran and then my sister went over to the door and locked it, and they went away. I was really frightened. This is a true story. And I bet that I will never go answer the door at night again." (Tamila Shalon).

*****

"It happened at Tam baseball field. The game was Marin City Boys Club versus Mill Valley Red Sox. In the first inning the Boy's Club got one run. And then the Red Sox came up to bat. And they bombed the Marin City Boy's Club pitcher and that was Carl Freeman. Two teammates Michael Evans and Alvin Hall said quote: "They bombed his black ass." A boy on Mill Valley hit a ball so far that you couldn't see it. A teammate said in his mind, "That old fat bastard can't pitch. All he is doing is throwing balls high and low." They said every inning he walked about two or three. Michael Evans, quote: "I'm surprised that the big black ass nigger didn't cry. From what Howell saw that black bastard can't pitch." Geary said, "His blackass is fucked up." Bettina said, "That Carl is not worth a shit in the game." (Hal).

*****

"Last night my sister and I went to a store called Safeway across the street from Tam High School. Well after we had went into the store these two hippies went into the store and they went back into the place where the ladies cash the checks and one of the man or hippie started looking around the store while the other man went over to the cash register and pulled out a gun and tried to hold up the store and one of the clerk grabbed him from behind and the hippie called out for him to help him. But the man just stood over him and looked. Two policemen came in just in time because the other hippie was getting ready to pick up the gun and the policemen grabbed him and took them away. And outside the store some more men were waiting for them to come out of the store but when they saw those policemen came in so they took off and never came back." (Little Green Man).

*****

"I was absent yesterday. Why? Because a dumb thing came and pulled our hill down over the road so it couldn't see. Cars . could not go by because the hill was too heavy to move and a tree was sitting right in the middle of it. Dumb. Well, the hill was soooo heavy that it spread out all over a neighbors hill and carport with little bushes clinging to the top for dear life. The bottom of the hill got sad and cried mud all over the road so nothing, with wheels could drive on it without slipping off the edge. (A milk truck did, and blocked cars, even though none come on our road). We, the people of Wellesley Ave. decided the mess needed to be removed so a bulldozer was called to try and move everything. He came late and when he tried to clean the mess, our road got even muddlier and there was danger of another slide. Everyone was very nervous about that and some left their cars at the other end of the road so in case more of the hill fell, they could, walk to their cars and try to swim out. Thats why I was absent yesterday." (Vouix).

*****

"I went to an open house at Lick-Wilmerding High School, which is a private boy's school in San Francisco. There were some nice people there. There were some punks there. There were some awfully queer kids there too.

I met one kid (okay) who kept trying to impress me by telling me about all the dope at the school. And how cheap it is. And what he can get for me and I kept trying to tell him that I wasn't worried about getting dope. That I could get it cheap enough but would he listen? No, he just kept on rapping, on on on about this dope and the kids who come up to you in the halls and say, "Hey kid, wanna' buy some hash or grasses or acid? mescaline? opeam? dexadrine? silociban? meth? Morphine? speed? smack? Pheneoborbitol? gas? rabbit shit? reds? celery points? beans? Hurry up I ain't got all day." (Adam).

*****

"My big sister Angel is very pretty, nice and sweet, in other words you could say, sugar and spice everything nice. When I went over to her house I asked if I could bring a friend along and she said that it was O.K. Friday, after school, we got a ride home with Mr. and Mrs. Butler, the car was crowded but the ride was not that long. That night we went out to dinner at the Copper Penny. After dinner we walked and looked at the town, then we went home and played records and set wigs. After we met her roommate, took a shower, and went to bed. On Saturday, cooked breakfast, took a shower, got dressed, and went shopping. We bought different things. We were going to see Putney Swope, but my friend and I couldn't get in so we went to shoot some pool. I didn't know how to play but I learned and real fast I won one game. We went home and played gin rummy. We stayed up till 4:00 in the morning and didn't get up till 12:00 that morning. I was really tripping." (Puddingtang).

*****

"I went to an old French movie tonight. I was standing by the candy counter near the door. There was a small black kid about eight years old standing about three feet into the theatre. I smiled at him and he smiled back and said, "Hi?." After a while he said, "How much do it cost to get in?" and I said, "Two twenty-five but you're already in," and he said, "Oh," and walk in to the movie house part.

At intermission, I went to the candy counter. They sold foreign chocolate. I bought two Milk Hazel-Nut bars went back to the movie, sat down gave him one and ate the other one. All through the movie I heard him silently crunching on it until he fell asleep. It was a good movie but I was thinking of my friend.

After it was over, I woke him up and asked him if his parents wanted him home. He looked a little scared and very confused. He didn't answer. I saw him head back into the theatre as I left. Someday I hope I meet him again." (Adam).

*****

"Yesterday I came home from school, and walking along the road to the beach, I noticed little sticky black globs of something that looked suspiciously like tar. Or asphalt. When I reached the beach, I saw that the parking lot was black-topped and had conspicuous CAUTION signs blocking the entrance. The parking lot goes almost up to the beginning of the beach and it has always been of dirt. People have nursed the thought that sooner or later the state would bust in and pave the place. A very disagreeable feeling. Well, I came bursting into the house pouring out all my feelings to Ma. Then Peter came home and raised the roof. He said that he was going to go down there at night and rip it apart with a mattock. He was really yelling his head off.

    Finally Pete called some person who usually knew what was happening and asked him what was happening with that asphalt down there. The guy said that it wasn't asphalt. So What was it? Pete wanted to know. It's oil. They oiled down the parking lot to pack the dirt together and control the dust.

   My brother proposed we all go down to the beach and see if the dude was telling the truth. He was. It was all gooky and wet and closed for three days. After awhile, the oil wouldn't look so dark. Feeling a little better, we all went home. No, wait. We went to the Muir Beach lookout first and ran back and forth along the cliff. Pa kept making such funny grunting noises when he ran, that I had to keep stopping and get my breath from laughing. We looked at the sunset. It was all over the clouds and in a tapering strip across the ocean. Then we went home." (New York, New York).

*****

"Last night I went to the Kingdom Hall of Jehovah's Wittiness. We sat down about four to five hours. My leg went to sleep and I kept hitting at it to make it wake up. So I didn't hear much of what went on. But when it was time to go I got up fast and started walking around so my leg would wake up." (Little Green Man).

*****

"Had a lot of fun yesterday. Robbie and I were walking home from school. The train was coming pretty soon so we stuck some little pieces of metal on the track so the train would stick them together. Suddenly, out of the sky, came Steve, in his smashing blue van and parked near the railroad tracks. We got in and talked for about an hour. Steve was having fun filling up his ego off of Robbie, for Robbie was actually acting in idiocy. It made him superior. Good ol' Steve. Well Robbie said the train was coming back. Let's stick some more shit on the tracks, so we did. Went back into Steve's car and talked some more.

   Reynolds came up in his car (Reynolds is a cop) and stopped. Steve had just told us he had quit dope. Reynolds came over and asked for his driver's license. "Pray tell, what for?" Steve asked.

Reynolds told us people saw us put stuff on the railroad tracks. We told him Robbie and I did. Reynolds took Steve's driver's license and went through all this fucking hassle to find out whether it was stolen or not. While Reynolds was at his car, Steve grabbed a pipe and stuck it under the driver's seat. "Damn liar!" was Robbie's reply. Well the car was not stolen, but Steve had a sixteen dollar parking ticket he didn't know about. Nice work.

You'd be amazed how much shit Steve has in his wallet. He opens it about twice a year to air it out and look through it. He's sitting finding all these pieces of paper with phone numbers on them. "Got to call them up someday, whoever it is." Some guy gave him a card up in a casino. Steve only met him once, but he'll call him.

Well, Steve didn't have sixteen dollars on him, so down to the station to book him. Sixteen dollars bail. Driving over Steve stuck some good tobacco in that pipe and got rid of the hash. Well, Robbie called his folks and got the money, but first we had to go to Robbie's house. A ten minute walk. First we went to the station to talk to him to make a deal about paying Robbie's folks back. Reynolds wouldn't even let us see him, wouldn't even give a ride up. Made it to the house in less than five minute. Grabbed the twenty dollar bill and ran to the station. Got there, Reynolds wanted change. Ran to the Caledonia Market, they gave a ten and two fives, no ones. Went to a gas station, got change for the five and ran to the station. Robbie pulled out the money, no ten. Nice; looked all over the neighborhood. A couple of cops we knew helped us look, Reynolds just told other people about it with a smile. Steve dug up another six dollars, put it together with the five dollar bill and the five ones and got out Steve. Steve said he'd pay Robbie for the ten he lost. But Robbie said something about he owed Steve ten anyway. Robbie owes his Dad 50, but he doesn't have to worry much about that. Spare change?" (Xathier X. Zeus).

*****

"The other day when we were picketing the *Independent Journal*, a guy comes up to me and says, "Do you work here?" indicating the I.J. building. "Hell, no. I don't work. I'm only 13. "Where did I go wrong," he says." (New York, New York).

*****

"Saturday I went to San Rafael and thought I was going to see a movie. Except that just happened to be the same day that I.J. strike was going on. I was about a show or two early, so I went around the corner to see what was going on. What I saw was a bunch of picketers walking up and down the streets with signs. I didn't want to get too close to the crowd because it was getting too large with angry people.

It was not too long before the tactical squad, and the police forces, moved in. They warned the people to move out immediately. But no one moved. So they called the first squad in, which pushed the people back into order. I only say the squad used violence once but that was enough, because alot of people were sent to the hospital. I feel that the people shouldn't picket unless they have a permit. Then things like that won't happen and they'll prove their point." (Edward).

*****

"It was 6:30. The clouds were still grey and separated with a faint moon in the distance. I lay down for a minute. When I looked up, the curtains were glowing slightly so I sat up. The sun was just rising, with a pink streak above the hills. Bright pink shown upon the clouds. The blueness soon grew deeper and the sun rose, giving the sky a golden color, silhouetting the trees against it. As I began to wake up, the grey slowly disappeared, leaving a yellowish clarity behind the hills and above me. Clouds passed the eucalyptus trees and sunk down out of sight, leaving the sun glowing. It was a huge golden ball that shone through the trees with transparent rays. It streaked across the sky; brightening quickly the mornings darkness which was once protected.

Shimmering drops of sunlight slither down, forming transcendent pools of smoothness against the bubbling trees. They bubble silently upon foaming rocks. The sky drips, slowly onto the blue horizon and dribbles into swirling rainbows." (Vouix).

*****

"About yesterday, I will give you a full detailed report. We were walking back from looking at the campsites which I wanted to see because I never had, when we came upon Mike, Howell, Alvin, Larry, Cathy, Rodney I think that's all. We stopped and asked them what they were doing and watched them run around. We were facing towards them when we saw something come flying towards us and land with a splat. We said "shit, what the hell'dya do that for?" then came another egg and we said "shit, cut it out." I saw Mike had another egg in his hand so I said, "Come on Laura, Mike has another egg." So we ran as fast as we could outta there. We went down to the waters edge and sat and talked until we were sure they were gone. We got up and left and started walking back when we saw Chocolate's car coming down the road. (By then we were worried about being late) we got in and she said, "Mr. Astons' so mad he's about ready to shit." So we went back and got in your car and got ready to jump out if you got in and turned around like you were going to hit us.

While we were riding along that old song came on the radio and Rodney started lip singing and we couldn't stop laughing. I think the only thing I really learned was not to be late. Not what Samuel P. Taylor Park is like." (Karen).

*****

"There is a dark blue sky
It looks beautiful as it reaches down
Touches the trees and hilltops
Then the sun comes up
And brightens the sky
The stillness of the morning

The sun rises from behind the mountain.
It slowly creeps up
A breeze blows a tree
And breaks the stillness
Its spring again
Flowers are coming out of their buds
The days are hot
And best of all
We're one season closer to summer
Summer, thats the season I want it to be
When its always so hot
and beautiful
Thats when we go up the mountains
Or out to the beach
And everyone you meet
Is so friendly
You meet a lot
Of really nice people
In summer
The memories of old friends
Are remembered best
With the return to old places.
A flower drops into a river
The gentle breeze blows it downstream
Who knows how far it will travel.
The wind ripples the green water
While the sun goes down behind the island
That is across the bay
Another day ends
As will another day begin." (Emily Marie).
****

11. Assignment: Today's News
Here are some copies of today's newspaper, make any comments you wish.

"The news of today is pretty bad. From what I read there's riots, killing, protesting, robbing, etc., etc., etc. But what got me is when they killed four kids at Kent State for no reason at all, and then they said there was a sniper on top of a building and he shot at the national guard so the national guard shot back and killed four kids. Then in Berkeley its the usual rock throwing, window breaking, fires, things burning, people getting kicked around, heads cracked, people getting shot, tear gas coming and going, just the usual protest day at Berkeley campus." (Ho Chi-minh Lennon).

*****

"Ohio. This time the national guard has gone too far. Their latest outrage (killing four students at Kent State, Ohio) is just too much! The latest development only tends to incriminate the guardsmen more.

They have proved that there was no sniper, that there was no order to fire, and that the firing was unprovoked! These four deaths were ones that hit hard all across the country.

President Nixon expressed sympathy to the parents but then tried to pull off another trick by blaming the students for the deaths. I believe that the President could show his sympathy by ordering all the flags to half-mast.

Cambodia--S.E. Asia. The President's latest move (into Cambodia) is unexcus- able. He moved into Cambodia without the O.K. of the Congress. He has moved to extend a war many people are against. He is moving in an effort to bring up the stock market.

Unfortunately for him soon after he moved into Cambodia the stock market plunged below the level it was after J.F.K. was killed. If the President believes we will be out of Cambodia by the end of June he is crazy.

One excuse will be found and then another, and another, and another....One excuse is that the enemy seems to have moved into Laos, so we will go in there. This war has got to stop!!!!!" (Simon).

*****

"Four people were killed at Kent State in Ohio by two policemen. The police or pigs should have shot up in the air three times for a warning. Some police shot at the ground and air.

Other police shot straight at the crowd killing four students. One of these days students are going to get together and buy plenty of rifles, and make bombs, and fight the pigs back. Some pigs take advantage of the students like pointing a gun at them, make them stop, then pull out a billy club and try to knock their brains out. Maybe next time you read the paper you'll read about four pigs shot instead of young women and men. Some pigs enjoy beating people with those clubs.

If I was a student I would fight back too. Maybe hide behind something and kill them just like they're killing us. I bet the pigs who shot one of those students is just living it up.

I'll agree that sometimes the students are in the wrong but mostly the cops are because they don't have to carry guns and rifles whatever just to stop a demonstration. At least they have hard helmets on to protect their heads from the rocks.

The students get hit on the bare head by a billy club. I'd rather get hit by one rock than go beat someone to death because of some rock throwing. They just can't go around killing just like you step on grass or ants or something.

Everybody wants to live a long life. The students don't have it their way and I don't blame them for fighting. They have to go to school and put up with kinds of things the police don't even know about. If one student was to sit down and talk to a policeman and tell him what it was all about he'll agree with you." (Jake Smoot).

*****

"It looks to me like the dawn of a revolution. Its going to build up worse and worse until it explodes. The government is going to crack down and the people are going to rise up. You can't just kill people without suffering a little and they are going to suffer a lot. I don't know what the present government will be replaced by. I hope its communism. That way we can stop pollution and people won't go hungry." (Adam).

****

12. Assignment: The Thematic Apperception Test

Psychologists sometimes ask their patients what is going on in these twenty pictures, would you like to try?

"This is an imagination or story telling test. You have been given a picture:
1. Describe what is happening in the picture.
2. Tell what the people in the picture are feeling and thinking.
3. Say what you think led up to this situation.
4. Say how you think it is going to work out.
When you have finished one picture you may exchange it for another if you wish."

My intent was solely to spur those kids who constantly say they can't think of a thing to write. I would not use the same pictures again, as their macabre nature influenced the responses. With subsequent classes I found any dramatic photos, taken from a magazine, served equally well.

———————

Picture 2.
"The picture is telling that the people have moved there and are starting a new world. The people are getting ready for the winter. The man is plowing the ground and the ladies are looking up and thanking God for letting them come to the new world. They are feeling good because they are very thankful to come to this new place, away from war. " (Dude).
*****
"The story probably's very sad; that she never returns to her dreams of that valley. It probably turns out that all she does, high on the mountain with her family, is just dream away. I think that she may just dream her life away. The people are caring and wondering only what tomorrow will bring. Something inside them wants to scream out to the world, "Help those who help themselves." (Somon Marie).
*****

"A Country Girl. I was born and raised in the country. I start school at seven and every day I come home I see these people and the mountain. Why do they keep following me? Barn yards, the beautiful crops and the two people in the background. Why couldn't I have been one of them? I guess I am what I am—a country girl. That's what I am." (Roger).

*****

Picture 3BM

"1. I don't know what led up to the event, but someone is either tired, crying or both.
2. A person is sitting on the floor with their head on a bench or chair.
3. The person is feeling sorry for someone or disappointed with something or someone. Maybe he's just tired or taking a nap.
4. If he is sleeping, when he wakes up he might go out and have some fun. If he is unhappy because of death he will overcome it. If his friends have become angry with him, he can find new friends." (Lynn).

*****

"A girl's parents have been killed in the war and her boyfriend was killed fighting in the war. The Germans had dropped bombs. The girl is thinking that everything is lost and she wants to kill herself. The girl will be captured by the Germans and finally die." (Jeffrey).

*****

"This picture shows a girl sitting with her back towards me on the ground with her head and arm resting on a couch or bench she looks as if she is either sleeping or crying.

Earlier in this day she was in a field with long flowering grass. The grass comes up to her knees and she runs while the wind blows the grass. The sun is low and sits on a hill.

The blackbirds fly to their homes in the trees where their young'uns sit chirping for their mothers to come home with some food.

When she tires of running along with the wind she sits in the grass and her head can barely be seen above the grass. She watches the sun sink behind the hills.

When the sun has gone down she walks to her home where her young1uns are crying for their mother to come home with some food.

She comes home without anything to eat so her young1uns will starve and she will starve too.

Now she is crying for she has been out enjoying the beauty of the world outside and her young'uns, who are now just wee babes will never see this sight for they will die and she is very sad.

God will look after this family of four. This mother and her three babes and they will somehow make it. She will take them to the field. The birds will fly and the wind will blow the grass and the sun will set. She will carry her babes in her arms then she will set them down and they'll watch the sun set." (Janie).

*****

"She sits there too stunned to cry but overcome with grief. Her father has been killed in a crash, on an airplane accident. Earlier we had seen the two policemen approaching her house slowly and solemnly. She opened the door for them not knowing, not expecting what they were about to say. As they told her the news she stood not believing a word but in her heart she knew it was true. As she closed the door behind them she slowly sank to the floor." (Dusty).

*****

Picture 3GF

"This poor lady has just slammed her finger in the door. Poor girl. She had a party and everybody got ripped off of their ass. When it got late nobody wanted to leave. So, she went to the door and slammed her finger in the door-on purpose!. The people all came to the door to see what happened and she pushed them out of the door. After she got them out she slammed her finger in the door again and again! Soon she became a door addict and lived bloody fingered for ever after." (Lief Erickson).

*****

"1.The woman is holding on to the door and she is crying because she is hurt.
2. She is hurt because her husband left her alone in the house.
3. She is feeling very bad because her husband left her alone.
4. She is going to kill herself because her husband did not come home and went to see another lady." (Francis).

*****

Picture 3GF
"Mrs. Elvoroys smiled warmly as her cherished husband and son, after working all day in the fields, ate heartily at the meal she had cooked. As they ate she stared at them and thought of when she married her husband and that she would do anything for them, for they were the only thing she lived for. Though not very wealthy, she made the best of everything, never complaining.
"Mary, honey, that was very good," said her husband.
"Mary?" "Oh, oh, yes, thanks.," she said as she started to clear the table.
 All of sudden she heard a crash. She ran over to see her husband lying on the floor, pale as a ghost. She started to cry and knew she had to get a doctor then she heard her son say....
"Mama, I feel hot and not so good" said he. She hastily put him in bed wrapped him up in three or four blankets. She got her husband and put him on the couch with some blankets, too. She ran outside, hitched some horses, and rode 10 miles to the nearest town. She ran around asking for the doctor, but no one would listened, then she remembered that no one ever spoke of the Elvoroys because of her being an orphan long ago from Europe, so people from when they were married, never spoke of them. The Elvoroys were going to move to the west when they made enough money. She screamed and lay on the dirt ground for help of her family, no one listened.

So, she rode back to the house swearing she'd pay them back someday. She walked in the door to the couch. Her husband barely alive and son dead from plague that had been going around. She knelt down near her husband, and he said in a whisper, "Take the money and go....to a place where you can live in peace." She held him and sobbed with his last breaths of life.

She felt him breath no longer. She had lost everything and didn't want to live. She staggered over and took a knife and stabbed herself and died in the arms of her husband." (Rabbit Paranoia).

*****

"In this photo the poor lady has been put out of her house by her husband. She wants to go back in so bad, but she doesn't know what to say. She is feeling very sad, and she is crying. It ends up that she goes back inside and she and her husband make-up." (Bettina).

*****

Picture 3GF

"1.This girl had a terrible fight with a friend who she cared about a lot. The friend went out of the house leaving her by herself. 2. She is crying because this person has left her and now she is all alone. 3. He will return the next day to get his things and she will try and follow him. The friend will only push her aside because he has no use for her and wants no part of her. She will return to the house, look it over and see how lonely it is, pack her things to go live in town."(Wildflower Weed).

*****

Picture 4

"The woman is trying to talk to the man and trying to make love to him. The man saw this girl making love to another boy and he is going to get him and she is trying to stop him by kissing him. The woman is thinking about love and the man is thinking about fighting. The man is going to kiss the woman and then go get that boy." (Chuck).

*****

"It was a dark and stormy night, and the waves tossed the ship wildly. Meanwhile back in New York city on South Street Mrs. Hazel Fogie was trying to fall asleep, but the wind, the rain, and the cats were keeping her awake. She was very frightened by all these noises. She tried humming herself to sleep but it didn't work. Then she tried thinking about her school years. She was right in the middle of a fight she had in sixth grade when she heard a loud noise in her living room. She gasped. Then, silence. She lay there for what seemed like hours, her heart pounding like a kettle drum. What should she do? Lay there or go see what it was? If it was a burglar, he might harm her if she found him, but he might come in her room anyway. She decided that since she was getting on in her years, that it didn't really matter if he hurt her. So, she got slowly out of bed and put on her robe and slippers. She tiptoed to her bedroom door and opened it ever so slowly. She peered around the wall. She gasped, there he was, whoever he was, and he heard her gasp, he spun around and pulled out a knife and threw it. There was a scream and he ran. Then silence." (Karen).

*****

"Marty and Marie. It was a hot night and Marty had her in his arms and she hugged him back but she brought up something about going to Europe and he turned her loose and turned away from her. She was still, hugging him and suddenly he said, "look, we have been all over that place. I'm tired of travelling. Can't we settle down somewhere?" Then she said, "Alright, alright!" They went into the living room for some ice cream." (Jake Brown).

*****

"A lady who love a man and wants him to stay with her and they look like they just came from in the bed and he is mad. He thinks she is just another girl. He is going to tell her he is going out." (Allan).

*****

Picture 6BM

"Mrs. Simms looked out sadly from the window. Her son (the long haired hippy) just died. In his relentless search to expand his consciousness and find, god he discovered a mushroom, amanita muscaria, the fly agaric. After eating this mushroom, which he had read that some Siberian peoples used to get "high", he began to hallucinate. Then he became very stimulated and broke out in a cold sweat.

He came home to his mother. There were severe pains in his intestines. He began to vomit. His mother, Mrs. Simms, immediately called her first son, the doctor, who hurried over. He was too late. His brother was dead.

She cried for a little while and then her son said, "Gosh, Mom, I sure am sorry but he wouldn't have amounted to anything anyway." (Adam).

*****

"The man tells his mother he is going to die in six months from drugs. His mother can't believe her son would do something like that. It ends up that the lady dies of shock and the man hasn't died as of this day." (Valerie Valias)

*****

'It looks like the man is besides his mother and his father has died. It is sad for the man but harder on his mother. The father was a detective and he got up to a murderer and the murderer killed the old man. The old lady is thinking he was too old to be doing a job like that. The man is thinking, "I'm going to get the man that killed my father. The old lady will get another old man and die sixteen years later. The boy will catch that man that killed his father and do him in." (Jeffery).

*****

"Well, this lady is sad because her son (right) has to leave for Vietnam and she won't have anybody to care for. They are in silence and thinking of all the good times of the past. She is hoping that her son will not get killed in the war. They are both sad from the day he was born up till now. They are hoping that they will see each other again. After this scene the son will leave with a sad goodbye." (Confucius).

*****

"A young girl, in her twenties, was sitting on a couch. Her mother had made her come to this beastly party, but that didn't mean she had to dance! She sat there, sulking. She noticed her mother giving her disapproving glances, but she ignored them. A man, in his mid-thirties, touched her gently on the shoulder. He had a pleasant face, his hair was gray, thinning, and he was smoking a pipe. The girl rather liked his presence and the smell of the tobacco smoke.

He had been watching her proud face for a while and decided to ask this pretty, headstrong girl for a dance. She seemed fairly shy. She was looking at him. He searched her face for some sign. Her pretty face was blank. "Would you like to dance?" Did her face light up at all? She looked at him, glanced at her mother and saw she wasn't looking. I'd love to." she said, after she was certain her mother didn't see her.

A little while later, on the hotel balcony, she told him how she disliked dances. He was sympathetic. They looked inside and saw, above the swirling dancers, her mother, looking both suspicious and triumphant as she watched them. "How .long has she been there?" she asked in despair." (Eleanor Hume).

*****

"A lady is sitting down and out of nowhere a man appears to be watching her. The lady was probably invited as a guest to someone's house and the person probably had to leave the room for something. While she was gone the man appeared. That lady probably didn't know he was watching her until she turned around. When she saw him he probably frightened her and she is probably thinking, "If only I could get out of this house and away from this funny looking man." The man could have been thinking that she is a very nice looking lady. That man could be making it very uncomfortable for the lady and the man is probably feeling very good in her presence. She probably leaves the house and never returns. After that I wouldn't either." (Somon Marie).

*****

"Tammi is a 20 year old girl who is very much in love with a boy by the name of Steve. Tammi thinks very much about him. He is nice and kind to her and she is nice and kind to him. One Saturday morning Tammi is waiting for Steve to pick her up so they can go to the theatre. Steve drives up and says, "Come on, let's split. The movie starts at 1:30 and its 1:20. Anyway, I have some questions to ask you." Tammi jumps in excitedly, thinking that he is going to pop the question to her.

"Tammi," he asks, "have you... ever... had sexual intercourse?'" "No I haven't and why do you ask me such questions about sex and that kind of stuff? It, and you, make me sick, now take me home." "O.K., I'll take you home, but I only asked because I want you to marry me, and have my children, and also clean my house, and I also love you Tammi."

"Oh Steve, I love you too, but I don't like the way you asked me that, and you know I never went out with any boys before I met you at the mayor's victory dinner and dance." "O.K., let's go to the theatre and you can sleep on the marriage questions." And they went to the theatre to see Planet of the Apes and Butch Cassidy and the Sundance Kid.

They got married, had three children, and lived happily ever after." (Love Bug).

*****

"Someone in the family might have passed and she thinks about it and sees him smoking a pipe. She is very surprised and maybe wanted to see him but not so soon. After the picture fades away she will probably tell everyone that she saw him again or, if she is superstitious, she will tell them that he has returned from the dead." (Puddingtang).

*****

Picture 7BM
"A lawyer and his client are talking. The client is mad. He wants to sue his wife for divorce. The lawyer is trying to talk him into not suing.. The client's wife ran out on him and wrote bad checks so he is mad about that. The lawyer talked him into helping his wife and not sewing." Randy).

****

"To me it seems as though they are talking about some business and also that it is very important. They look as though the world is coming to the end and they're about ready to cry. The reason they'll cry is because they won't be as rich as they thought they were going to be." (Edward).

*****

"Richard Nixon and Grandad talking it over. Nixon is pushing heroin and Grandads gonna buy some." (Harry Bippo).

*****

Picture 8BM
"A man and a boy were walking in a forest and someone shot the man and when the suspect saw the boy he ran. But he dropped his rifle. The boy ran to the nearest house to get help. The boy came back with the men who said they would help. On the way to the house the-men found the rifle and took it with them.

The men were cutting him open making the boy think they were going to extract the bullet. The boy was feeling very sad and the men were plotting. One of the men went over to the boy and told him the man died and just then he stabbed the boy with great force." (Fritz the Cat).

*****

"That man right before the other man is an unconscious soldier who gave his life for this country. Why can't we have love, peace and good will for all men and women? . Why can't someone help me and other people to face life without a broken arm or no legs at all? For God's sake someone help me to be what I want to be. Come on America please help your men in Vietnam." (Roger)

*****

Picture 9BM

"Wow man! (pronounced "mawn"). A bunch of speed freaks listening for rabbit tracks on the floor of their apartment. They had three joints a piece and tonight they got a bunch of chicks coming over, but the way they look I don't think that they'll be able to do anything once they get there.

They only have one pair of underwear each, because they pawned their other pairs to buy dope (far out) to get bombed out on. They will die at the age of ninety because they had such a healthy and happy childhood." (Harry Bippo).

*****

"A group of hoboes sleeping. They had been on the road all day and were tired so they're sleeping. All of the people are tired. They had a hard day travelling, running out of town because of an anti-vagrancy ordinance. They are about to be picked up by the county police for loitering. They'll be thrown in jail and when they get out they'll be told to either get a job or get the hell out of the county." (Washington Irving).

*****

Picture 10

"Well, it's about this love affair with each other and they're both married with different people. But they don't want to leave each other, so in the picture they're talking about how they love each other and they want to get married. What happened in the end is they went to another country and got married to each other and lived until they died." (Fu Man-chu).

*****

"Someday he and I will be together. All that is in my head is loving him. I hug him, he can hug me and we will get married. Thinking of getting married, having a baby and feeling love." (Clayton).

*****

"Well he's late she thought. It seems like he's always late or always early--sh, here he comes. The door opened. In the semi-darkness she could tell he was smiling by the reflection of light off the high cheek bones.

"Hello," she said. "Hi," he said, still smiling, "Do you have the money?" "I've...I've decided not to give it to you." She saw the cheekbones drop. "Why you little...," he said, advancing toward her. Then he stopped suddenly, as if to correct himself. "Why my dear sister, you've never objected to giving me money before." He took her in his arms and gave her a hug. She could almost feel his thoughts burning into her mind. Back to the time he first brought the news that her real brother was dead. Back to the time when he offered to be her new brother--for a price, and now he was asking for more money. She picked up a nearby pipe she had put there earlier.

"If you insist on not paying me I'll have to kill you dear." She brought the pipe down on his head with a dull thud. She dumped him head first out of the window and waited until she heard the unmistakable crack of a skull on the pavement. She then sighed and put down on her shopping list; "1 new brother." (Potassium Nacnud).

*****

Picture 11

"The fog was lifting. Elaine could feel the weight of the darkness getting less. She and Paul were lost in the wood. They had found an old road and, leaving Jeanette in the camp, they had followed it. Dave was gathering firewood at the time.

Elaine and Paul had taken off, yelling to Jeanette that they would be back in a couple of hours. The road they were on was gravel and the valley was shrouded in gravel-colored mist. The fog was lifting now. They'd be able to see where they were soon. The valley was brighter now. The trees were back aways. A little way up the hill there was a stream. It went halfway down the hill and then went underground. They were standing on a bridge, an arch between two hills. It was completely stone and it was about 200 feet up.

"Paul," Elaine cried, "Look down, almost directly below. Its our camp!" "You're right. I wonder if there is a way down!" The two of them dropped their jackets down to the camp and began to scramble down. At first it was easy going but it narrowed down to almost sheer cliff at points. They got down to about 75 feet with no mishap, then, Paul began sliding, he couldn't stop himself. He was bringing rocks down past him and on down the hill. About 35 feet below him it went into a cliff for a 40 foot drop. He stood up on the slide as it went on down. About 5 yards from the edge there was a tree. If he could get to it he would be safe.

He was about 3 feet from it and he jumped. He grabbed a branch with one hand and his other arm circled the trunk. He was safe! Then he saw Elaine. She was pinned by the slide. He let go of the tree and tried to reach her. She went over the side of the cliff still pinned! Paul went over the edge. He found Elaine. She was dead. The slide had crushed her skull.

Jeanette and Dave came up. They saw Elaine. Silently the three of them started to dig a burial pit." (Washington Irving).

*****

Picture 12F

"While this overjoyed person is admiring himself thoroughly his godmother is about to pour strawberry jam down his back. She has labored over it all week and is very pleased at herself for being so daring. In fact, so completely surprised is she for being so naughty, she is virtually oozing with jam.

As she gets ready to perform this unheard of act, the jam, which she has carefully concealed in her left pocket, begins to drip rapidly, tickling her. It squiggles under her feet and toes making standing still impossible until she finally hurries away, giggling heartily and leaving the great admirer to himself, unaware of the great peril he would have been in." (Vouix).

*****

"The old lady is trying to smell the man. To see how he smells--good or bad. She would just like to smell him because she likes to smell men. To me old ladies always do something funny. He is thinking about the girl but she is thinking about how he smells. I think he will walk away from her and she will follow him because she thinks he likes." (Penny).

*****

Picture 12M

"The Internal Revenue Service and the junkies were really after this man laying down. They were after him so much that he decided he wanted to die. In here the man is trying to die and a spirit comes and tells the man to follow him. The spirit is trying to get him to follow and the man is kind of afraid to follow. It turns out that the man decided he has the will to live and the spirit goes away. The junkie was really getting down the man's back and so he took some heroin. He got busted and was sent to Napa." (Valerie Valias).

*****

"Keith always envied Leon for being so smart all the time. He wished that he could be smart too. One night while Leon was sleeping, Keith snuck in and hit him with a flounder. While he was out Keith took all of his knowledge and replaced it with his own. He then hid the flounder under a loose floorboard and went to sleep.

That morning Leon awoke and was just as smart as before. Keith woke and was very smart. They lived happily ever after. Why? The reason they were both smart is that the flounder (see "flounder") was smarter than both of them (see "smart") and so when Keith hit Leon all of the flounder's brains went into Leon's head. The flounder is now a vegetable and trying to get out from under the floorboard." (Lief Erickson).

*****

"A little boy is sitting, thinking, or maybe even dreaming. Dreaming of a better world, a better place to live, a place of peace and happiness. A place where he doesn't have to be hungry or even think of the word "hungry," or "sadness," or even "loneliness." But this little boy knows he is just dreaming and he had better wake up soon because he knows that this will never happen." (Shirley).

*****

"He sits alone with nothing to do, nowhere to go, no one to play with. Feeling sad and lonely, wanting someone to be with. His mother and father died leaving him alone wanting a friend." (Laverta Jean)

*****

"Stuart sat wistfully staring into the red glare of the sinking sun. Papa had promised to be home at noon. Stuart thought of the new boots his father was bringing him. If Papa spent his boot money on whiskey he would run away from home. He had told all the other migrant worker's kids about his new boots and if Papa didn't get them he would be so embarrassed. He bit his lip. Papa was driving up the road in the Studebaker. The old dented car shined in the descending sun. The car swerved uncertainly from side to side. He let out a disappointed sigh, wiped the blinding tears from his eyes and turned to go inside. His sister met him at the door.

"Is he back yet?" she asked and noticed the tear streaks on Stuart's cheeks. All Stuart's hard earned money! "I told you not to trust him," she said, putting her arm around him. "We'll earn some money somehow." She thought of the hours Stuart had spent earning that money and said sadly, "Sometime " (Eleanor Hume).

*****

"Lost in the Shadow: Lost in the shadow of darkness never to face life and reality again never to face manhood again here I will stay and watch time pass away. Hallucination and dream's nightmare come true in a new world of light and day Difference is related.

Why did it have to be me? I was the good man whenever my mother wanted me I came. Why did it have to be me? Why Lord? Its always the lonely people of the shadows between life and death and day and night." (Roger).

*****

"The curiosity of a little child. Climbing up stairs to see where they will lead to. He is wondering what excitement he will find at the top, then will he come skipping back down again to look for something else." (Emily Marie).

*****

"104, 105, 106, 107, 108, 109, 110, 111, 112, 113, 114,115, 116 , 117, 118, 119, 120 , 121, 122, 123 , 124…." (Karen).

*****

"The man and the lady are poverty stricken and someone is knocking on the door, so the man gets up to answer the door. The lady is thinking she loves the man and all the man thinks is that he is too tired to answer the door. It was the man collecting the rent at the door. The people can't pay so they get kicked out into the street." (Valerie Valias).

*****

"A woman is laying in the bed with no clothes. The woman is thinking about sex and the man is scared from seeing the woman in bed naked. The woman will talk to the man and ask him what is wrong with him and then she might ask him to get in the bed with her and make love." (Chuck).

*****

"Well it started a month ago when she wanted a baby and they had an argument on not having and having a baby. A few weeks later when they were in bed she got up and took off her clothes and said she wanted to have a baby, so he got up put on his clothes and left her in bed and he walked out on her. After a few hours he went back home thinking about having a baby. When he got there she was crying so he asked her why she wanted to have a baby and she told him that she wanted a baby so she can take care of it. So he gave her a baby and lived till he got married." (Fu Man-chu).

*****

"There was a man who went on a trip out of town and he left his woman at home. She was at home in the bed when a prowler came in the house when she was in bed and the prowler killed her. When the man came home he found her in the bed--dead." (Stanley).

*****

"What a fine b-t-h he had for dinner! I'd be holding my head too if I had as busy a night as he did. The girls' out cold because she had 13 too many martinis. Oh well, to each his or her own. What a mother……. blast he had.

Mr. Aston, don't let Mom and Dad read this (I had 6 too many martinis) or else they shall very politely take me apart.

Oh well, that cat sure had himself a night but that ain't my business, so I'll leave him in his predicament now (wondering how he's gonna get the money to pay her!)

Thus ends my small little look at America. I would like to thank my brain in telling my hand to hold my pencil and move it so it could write on this here paper." (Harry Bippo).

*****

"In town he was thrown out of a bar while getting into a fight. He was then caught stealing a can of beer in a grocery store. Then he was arrested on a charge of disturbing the peace but was out of jail when his ex-wife paid to get him out.

He is thinking now what is left in the world. Why is he not being treated like a human being. He will next jump off the highest rooftop in the world to his doom." (Confucius)'

*****

"A man having a view of the city and he is thinking about a girl, where she is and what she is doing, and he sees a girl that looks just like her but it is not his love. So, he takes a big breath of air and just sits there and goes on with what he was doing when he thought about his problems and he was sad he was not thinking about his girl friend." (Allan)

*****

"A man who was in prison started hollering, pretending like he was sick. The guard came and opened the door. He had made a gun out of some wood and held him up. He is getting ready to escape through a small window, thinking if he should do so or not. He is thinking if he will have a better life out in the world.

He escapes and goes and finds out that things have changed since he was in prison. He also found out that people were talking behind his back. So, he goes back to jail on his own free will and said he will be satisfied where he was." (Kimberly).

"Inside looking out at the world through a broken window. The darkness of the world and the coldness. But inside the window it is warm." (Emily Marie).

*****

"The picture is in the graveyard. It is now judgement day, the time for all people, dead or alive, to come before the great Johovah. The first one to come up was a man on the devil's side. He was the first because he was the meanest one of them all. Now it is time for him to go, he must stand alone. He takes his last look at the graveyard because he know that was going to be his last time there. From then he just vanished. And so did the rest of the bad people." (Little Green Man).

*****

"The guy in the picture is praying over the grave of his son who was killed in Vietnam. He is very saddened by the loss and is praying for his son to go to heaven. Around him are the graves of many other soldiers who were killed fighting for their country.

On the headstone of the grave it reads, "Here lies Johnny Brut. He got a bullet through his gut." Some of the other headstones read, "Here lies Jonathan Rimole, he picked a pimple." Or, "Beneath this stone, a lump of clay, lies Uncle Peter Daniels who, too early in the month of May took off his winter flannels." Or, "Here lies Jonathan Snake, he stepped on the gas instead of the brake." (Harry Bippo).

*****

Picture 17GF

"The girl lives in this ancient castle with a moat around it. One of the prisoners whom he liked has escaped and she is out on the ramparts hoping to catch a glimpse of him. The girl is out there hoping to see the man so that she can help him escape over the moat. She is thinking only of trying to help him and not of how much trouble she might be in. The outcome is that she is caught and punished severely for her evil thoughts by her father." (Wildflower Weed).

*****

Picture 17GF

"I'm not sure but it looks like a plantation. One reason why it might be a plantation is because of the slaves carrying sacks some place with the slave master standing over them. I might be mistaken but that's what I thought." (Stuart).

*****

"A lone child contentedly polishes and cleans her domain. Alone, with the sun and clouds her companions. In front of her a cool blue river ambles by, shimmering with mid-day sun. Wood, just polished, shines richly with warmth she has given it. Alone, a breeze ripples the water and she floats away." (Vouix).

*****

Picture 18BM

"I don't know what lead up to this. A man may be in a cold sweat from singing and someone may be taking his coat off, or trying to sit him down. This man may be thinking about someone, judging from the look on his .face. If he is thinking about someone who left him he'll forget it." (Lynn).

*****

"This here cat is putting on his coat inside out. He has a double jointed arm! He also has three of them! He got stoned drunk on the night of February 17 on a Tuesday. The year 1902. He had one too many martinis and now he's going home to get yelled at by his ever lovin' old lady." (Harry Bippo).

*****

Picture 18GF

"Jessica ran from house to house. Hiding among the shadows. She heard the far off shrill of a siren. Chills ran through her body. She saw the light shining through the window of a house. She swung around to the back of the house and quietly opened the door. Softly walking she made her way through the kitchen to the living room. She was home again. How good it felt after being locked up in the asylum, just to be able to go anywhere she wanted. She wanted to stay free always. But as she walked into the light of the living room, her heart no longer had pleasantness in it but it filled with rage. Her husband sat on the couch with him, the woman who had taunted and had forced her husband to commit her to the asylum. Jessica approached them steadily her eyes filled with hate. John looked up and saw her and he knew she had the will and power and hate to kill Rebecca. He swiftly caught up Rebecca, giving her instructions to run. She started for the door but Jessica, caught her, grabbing her around the neck she squeezed with all her might. This woman would no longer taunt her. John pulled at her arms but they did not weaken their grip. They squeezed on. Rebecca slowly sank to the ground. Dead.

Jessica realized what she had done but she could not break now. She must run, forever she would run." (Dusty).

*****

"There is a murder being done. Why is it being done? Well, it is a long story turned into a short story. It all started by the girl who is being murdered. She started going with the other girl's boy friend. The other girl got mad and decided to kill her. So, she called her over to her house and killed her." (Laverta Jean).

*****

"The man was mad at the lady and running down the stairs after her he slipped and konked his head on the banister. The man is dying and the lady ran back and tried to comfort him. The lady is thinking that she's sorry she stole the man's money and the man is unconscious. The man dies and the lady falls on him crying." (Valerie Valias).

*****

"In this picture (to me) it looks as if a person is killing another person by choking them. To me I think the killing might have started by an argument or the person being choked did somethingmnthey had no business doing, or maybe the person that is doing the choking is going crazy. There are lots of reasons why this person is killing the other person. The reason why I am saying person all the time is because I don't know if these two people are men or women.

In this picture the person who is doing the choking is thinking, "I'm going to kill her no matter what happens." Then again it looks as if the person is thinking he or she killed my brother, now I'm going to kill him. It looks as if this situation is going to be first degree murder." (Doris).

*****

A girl came home after she had been out for a week and her parents tried to talk but she cussed them out. So, her mother grabbed her ears and beat her. When she had finishes d she took her to the doctor and found out she was pregnant and then went to an unwed mother's home." (Hugh).

*****

Picture 20
"He shuffles quietly down the empty street, heavy with thick mist. Not a flicker of life stirs. The road gets very narrow. He walks on. Suddenly, the road narrows and stops, ending in a thin V-like crevice. Everything stops. He peeks through a small crack revealing light, meadows and sky. Life. He turns. Nothing. Turning, grasping, there is nothing. The silent empty body of his flows upward. (Vouix).

****

13, Assignment: On the Death of a Seagull

Yesterday a seagull was killed in the school yard. This is not the first time. What do you feel about this? Does this have anything to do with social studies?

───────

"You are supposed to be teaching about history and the present things. I don't think talking about seagulls, death and murder has anything to do with social science because social science is the study of history and six other things I can't think of the name of." (Lynn).

*****

"The reason why people kill is because they're stupid, dumb, insane and probably don't know what life means to them or anybody else. Anybody who can look at something dying, kill something, anything, and to watch it die and lose its life, or kill for no reason is really unbelievable and that person must be really weird in the head.

Can we live without killing another man? I guess not because it is going on all the time and its officially O.K. at war. There should be a law against killing anyone or anything." (Rabbit Paranoia).

*****

"I don't like seagulls at all because you can't even make one step without them dropping on you. If I could get away with it I would try to kill them all. I think its fun throwing rocks at seagulls as long as you don't get caught." (Henry).

*****

"This is a very depressing thing. I feel sorry for the students because to do something as brutal as this they must have had, or felt they had, been treated similarly. Neglect maybe. I'm sure their actions may have some connection with the way they were brought up. They didn't hate the seagull but I would say they were taking it out on it.

Well, on second thought maybe they were. I wish they could of found something more amusing to do. This is a hard subject to write on." (New York, New York).

*****

"I don't care if the seagulls get killed because they don't have anything to do with my education. I don't think this has a damn thing to do with what you are supposed to be teaching." (Janie).

*****

"The reason why I think this happened is because people throw the food they don't want on the ground. When that happens the seagulls start coming in with heavy artillery, you all know what that is, B.M., manure. So, when a student gets B.M.'d on the best way they get revenge is by throwing rocks and hitting them. Another reason is they throw at the seagulls for target practice. They do that just for kicks." (Edward).

*****

"I don't care about these seagulls. They ain't got nothing to do with our education! Anyway they don't do nothing but fly around dropping turds on people's heads!" (Ella).

*****

"The seagull was killed because people don't give a damn. The kid who killed it is probably bragging about it now. The last few seagulls killed have been hit by the same person.

It's not profitable to care about animals. The pelicans have almost hatched no eggs this year—score one more for capitalist pollution. The U.S. is trying to destroy a whole people because we make money. People are starving because people make money. Pollution might destroy us all but it isn't stopped because: people don't care, people make money, money is power."(Adam).

*****

"You are supposed to be teaching social science and how to learn. I do think that this (seagulls, death and murder) has something to do with social science because it deals with people, their minds, lives and government." (Vouix).

*****

"You are suppose to be teaching history and the government of the United States. I think that killing seagulls doesn't have anything to do with social science, but, I would much rather write about seagulls than to be bored learning about history, and besides, I want to learn about the present and the future instead of the past." (Doris).

*****

"Thats good for them greedy suckers. They always use the bathroom on people. I hate them anyway. They use the bathroom on the basketball court and all over every place. You can't even eat in peace without them things pestering people." (Stuart).

*****

"Lets say you're walking home with a group of your best friends who you know very well. As you are walking along you find a seagull who is mortally wounded. Now someone in your group says, "Hey, there's a mortally wounded seagull that we are about to pass."

O.K., now comes the critical part. While your friends are looking at it someone will say, "Let's stone it," or, "Let's save it." Whichever comes first is usually what your group does. And, because man has a bad nature, its usually the first statement that gets results." (Potassium Nacnud).

****

14. Assignment: Who are you?

"Tell me something about yourself. (I know you've done it before, but I would like you to try it again.) What turns you on? What turns you off? Do you feel good about yourself and the world around you? How do you feel on the inside? Are you who you seem, or are you keeping up a front? What one word describes you? Write a poem about yourself."

This was essentially a re-statement of the first assignment. By now, however, most of the students had become more open and were willing, to tell more about their inner lives.

"I wish, I wish
I wish I was nice
I wish, I wish
I was a queen
don't you?" (Francis).

*****

"How I Feel
The old and angry,
The new and old,
The good and the bad,
What's left beside?
Love and hate.
You love your friend,
You hate your teacher.
Why is it you hate your teacher
and love your friend?
You think you're so cool
When you're nothing but a fool.
Who can run around
and be so dumb." (Laverta Jean).

*****

"I feel shitty today and I hate everyone and everything. Last night was the first class of four sandal making classes. It was three hours long and all I did was draw the outline of my feet. Also yesterday I got two cavities filled and the Novocain hasn't worn off completely yet. Last Tuesday I got five filled. Last Thursday I got two filled. Yesterday I got two filled. Next Thursday I get one more filled. Last Tuesday was the first time I ever had Novocain. I've had fillings but never with Novocain. It felt very odd. Like my chin was dead.

Someday soon I'll talk to you about being a longshoreman but not today." (Karen).

*****

"A person can feel lonely in a really big crowd. But a lot of times I don't even want to be in a big crowd even if I'm not lonely. I just like to sit on a mountain and think. You really can get a lot of thinking done." (Emily Marie).

*****

"I'm not honest with myself. It's easier to lie and say I will be a hero. It's easier to say I will speak out--next week. If I'm not honest with myself, how can I act toward others. Like the person I think I am? No, that's where my dishonesty shows up.

I'm not afraid of whites. If I get in a fight with a white and get beat, okay. But I won't fight with a black. I'm too scared. The pain is the same.

Why am I scared to get up in front of a class and talk. I'm scared of being laughed at. Why is that so bad?

I'm not talking to the ones who aren't listening. They don't care about what I'm saying. I don't care about what they're hearing. I'm talking to the ones who do care. At this point it ain't for me to make anyone care. The ones who aren't listening, if somehow forced to listen, wouldn't do anything anyhow.

I'm scared of being heard. I'm scared of saying something meaningful to me and someone stepping on it, because it isn't meaningful to them.

Do I stop caring what people think? My whole way of work is based on what people think. As I said somewhere else, its prostitution. But how do you stop it? How do you learn to make your own judgements? What other people think matters.

Yeah, but not as much as people think, and base their action on. No, but it still matters in how you give a presentation, so you get the right idea across, but not in your own moral judgements. Then how do you make moral judgements?

Or, how you as a person, with what education on the subject, and what opinions you have, what you, weighing these with older convictions from your upbringing, think.

Aha, so it goes back to your parents, who brought you up. Not only your parents, but your friends and their friends, and everyone who influences you. It could be movie star, if that movie star is important to you. Probably your convictions will change from time to time.

This is important to me. I never before put it on paper, I never before thought it out to this extent. Watch your words Mister Aston, you're influencing my convictions." (Washington Irving).

*****

"What's right and wrong, good and bad, etc.
I am writing in Mr. Aston's Social Science Class. What about, I haven't the faintest idea. I'm bored and I don't know what in the world I'm supposed to do about it. Nothing to do except think about the weekend and what I'm going to do while I'm out of class. It's Friday, but I don't really feel all keyed up. We were supposed to have a party this morning, but only me and a couple of other kids brought food, so there wasn't any party.

I'm down in the dumps thinking about the new schedule that comes into effect on Monday and I'm thinking what kind of golfer that I'm going to grow up to be. Blues got me down as far as I can go without going underground. I'm sorta hungry but I don't really feel like eating. I've just got the feeling this ain't gonna be my day. The music playing in the background just doesn't seem to help either.

I think more than half the class has got the same darn feeling that I do. Maybe they are a little bit more interested in things than I am right now, but I don't really think anybody is that keyed up. This is probably one of the quietest classes we've had all year. In my opinion, even though it may not be the quietest decibel wise, my mind is probably more quiet than it has been in any class this year.

Here I am just staring blankly into space thinking about how endless time really is. It's sorta weird to me that we are living in one minute period of time, that time has been going on forever and always will go on. When you really put your mind to it and think about it, you sort of wonder if there isn't really a catch about the whole doggone cycle of birth, life, death, and the hereafter, whatever the heck that might be.

This probably sounds so stupid you could throw it in the trash, but to me, its making just a little bit of sense. In my horoscope, it says that Scorpios (like Billy Graham) are supposed to have some pretty good guesses about life, death, etc., and sometimes come pretty close to guessing the truth.

I just got up to sharpen my pencil and found out that when I got back to my seat I completely forgot what the heck I was writing about. Forgetfulness isn't one of Scorpio's trade, but I just blew it, so I'll say, "Adios." (Harry Bippo).

*****

"The Hurt is Over. This is a story that happened to a person that I know. Its sort of a sad story.

There was a boy that came into the life of a friend. And he asked her to go with him and she said, "Yes." By the way, I will not mention any names. When the word got out that they were going together people were happy.

Now the couple didn't have any real bad things in their way. Everything was going so smooth. Now a friend of the couple came along, which was a girl. She kept on flagging the couple. Now the girl had interrupted the couple's relationship. Once the girl friend of the boy caught the other girl and her boy friend around a building. Now he would always come to the other sister of his girl friend and say that she was always listening to her other friends. Things started looking so bad that the couple had a lot of angry words in between them that they just broke up. Now that's why I am so very cautious that I just don't really have one to this very day. Now the other day she told, "You know that hurt is over and I've forgot all about it." (Somon Marie)

*****

"I'm so happy I've kicked the habit of smoking and I've also stop smoking weed and I feel much, much, better. I've been unhappy for the reason the boy that I really, really, love and me broke up. And another reason is that I've just been unhappy about my school work. I guess I'm just unhappy. But now I'm happy about one thing. I go back with the "I quit" and I'm so happy. I want to be free for a year just to see how I would live. But I wouldn't want to do this by myself. I feel love, I want love, I need love, and I give love, because I am love.

I dig music and art, those two things make me happy when I'm unhappy. Black is beautiful. I love flowers they smell so good. Have you ever seen a black flower?" (Shirley).

*****

"Have you ever been caught with a bag in your hand, just standing there, looking silly? Have you ever been just standing there, with burns in your face, with everybody looking at you? Just like that, with your mouth open." (Jake Brown).

*****

"I feel like dough thats been rolled over with a rolling pin. I feel like I am under a steamroller. I feel like I've been dropped off a 2,000 foot building and splattered on the rocks below. I've been trying to pick myself up, but one piece is over there and one is over here, and all is red and bloody. I feel like a lightbulb that's burning out with no thanks from any person. I feel like an eggplant that's been boiled, like a piece of used Kleenex, like something thrown away. I have a headache. I feel as though one thinks about me when I'm not there.

I've been brooding about how I can't talk to people about the things I think about. I've been wishing I could see things through another person's mind for a while to see what someone else thinks.

I don't want to write all I feel. I don't know how to describe how I feel. I feel like a sneer, like a headache, like pessimism. There's so much bullshit. How do you separate the bullshit from some grains of ideas and, if you can, how can you make other people do it; realize there is bullshit and realize that what's not bad or false is still possibly just mediocre or indifferent.

Learn, watch, listen. Hear what other people have to say. Listen beyond and behind words for the feelings of troubled people. I like being alone. The person who reads this will probably learn something about me. I hope someone reads it. I've got to live my life. No one can do it for me.

I'll walk my road. I'll rest by the way-side. I'll drink from a stream. I'll walk through a puddle. I'll skirt the road and walk through the woods. I'll gambol and leap through the meadows. But I won't turn back." (Washington Irving).

*****

"Lonely. Loneliness, is being in a world of your own. Without nobody. Just lost in the shadow of darkness without a human soul around. Completely in another world and time, possibly another planet. Out in the universe among the stars there is the smallest, coldest lonely planet Pluto. Where the Pluto God stands to awake you." (Roger).

*****

"Help! So I'm conceited. I know that I'm conceited. Even as I'm writing now, I'm writing like I am conceited. Now that I've got that sparkling bit of information what do I do with it. You said that I think I'm sophisticated. You're right, but fuck I can't even spell it. So you tell me how not to be conceited, but if you told me I wouldn't accept it because you are conceited. Some people make it a lot harder for me to accept it from. Grace tells all her friends and me how conceited I am, but it only makes me mad because I think she's worse than I am.

I sit here thinking that I know I'm conceited so it's not that bad. I talk to my friends about it and we're all feeling the same old way and acting the part, like hot shit.

So here's a test. You tell me how not to be conceited, and after you're through then you, who has been to some thirty countries in your life and have seen and read more than I probably ever will, tell me how not to brag. People are aggravated most by the things that other people do that they dislike in themselves. So if you're so fucking perfect you tell me what to do about it because I don't like it." (Adam).

*****

"I would like to be a bug so that I can be easily be crushed. Most of the time I don't feel good about myself. My smell is sour and sharp, my feel is hard and mean. Lots of time I put up a front. More and more I can't find myself. I am scared most of the time. Sick looking is my color, mostly all colors put into one line. My sound is a sound that keeps saying the same thing over and over again because I can't get the answer. The one word that describes me is "ugly". A man without love.

To escape, I dream of many strong things--things that lead me to many uncontrollable things. I feel I have some kindness that intercepts greed but not altogether stops it.

To escape from reality at night I test my nerve by going into creepy places. I'd rather die of fear than know me. I am mostly scared of myself." (Mao Nixon).

*****

"I feel that I am nice to people, Black or White. I feel that one day the world is going to come to an end." (Penny).

*****

"Fire Hydrant Blues. People have been walking all over me. I'm a bitching post. I feel like a barroom spittoon (drinks and emphysema on the house). I feel like a fire hydrant.

Have you ever felt like a dull gillette stainless razor that just finished shaving a turd? Or like the Berlin Wall? Or like the dirt in Vietnam? Or like a fly looking up from an outhouse? Or the sidewalk underneath the man who jumped from the fiftieth story? Or like a roll of toilet paper awaiting its doom?

Sometimes I feel this way and worse. When I feel this bad I like to listen to Neil Young, not because he makes me feel happy but because he sympathizes with me." (Adam).

*****

"Life is full of colors, Like a psychedelic Cadillac.
Black white and orange, All those deep forms
Of life." (Roger).

*****

"Its really funny how certain smells bring back memories. I have some cinnamon oil that I got in the summer and I used to wear it all the time. Just the other day I put some on and it made me remember all the things I did last summer. Some things can happen so quickly its like a dream. When you wake its all gone. Maybe you will have a few memories, but then you forget them.

When I. .get married it will be up on the mountain. The sun will be shining and the wind will blow. The white chiffon gown fluttering in the wind. Everyone will be happy, peaceful and joyous." (Emily Marie).

*****

"A Poem About Myself
Black as night.
Black as the cloth you wear.
Black is a color.
Black is a color that will never fade away." (Penny).

*****

"The Line: What is a line? Its you and I.
Its ugly and beautiful. Its happy and sad.
Its funny and serious. We are all the same." (Maria)

*****

"Clayton's Night: On the night of graduation. I am going to have some fun. I am going to be tripping all night long and have me some lady.

That night I am going to have every thing. I'm going to be in my Bad rags. jest stolling my back off. I am going to pay the teacher back because the treet me rong. Im going to put the tires on flat." (Clayton).

*****

"Always happy, Never sad.
Always friendly, Never bad.
Sometimes lonely, Never a cry.
Never a sad good-by." (Doris).

*****

"Reaching: Reaching is wanting. Wanting to have something or things, things you can't do or have. Reaching is your whole life. A lot of times it ends up with a big lump in your throat." (Rabbit Paranoia)

****

Boss man Boss

15. Assignment: Friends

Please tell me something about one of your classmates. How do they feel on the inside? Is there a sound or color that describes them?

    This was one of the most successful assignments given. Maybe the fact that it was a wet and dark winter morning had something to do with it, but never was the class so intent and quiet. They were so absorbed that, when the end of class bell rang, not one student stopped writing.

"...Her color is like a very pretty green tree in Autumn about to let the leaves fall." (Chuck).

*****

"Beautiful you are,
Brown is your feeling.
Sweet smell skin,
Silky is your hair.
Your deep looks like
 a beautiful blooming flower.
Your teeth are so white
as white as rice.
Beautiful chin, nice round nose, sweet unforgotten is your smile.
Calm you are at times, Beautiful, beautiful, I should say you are."
(Jake Brown).

*****

"There is someone
who loves me very much.
He sings this song
and it puts him down.
He tries to be
like the people of love.
To do what they do
to be what they are.
He like nothing

in himself
and is like a bird trying to be a lion.
He is like a flower
He is always smiling
When you see him
but inside all he feels is hatred." (Janie)

*****

"This person thinks that they are good looking and they think they can get away with about anything and deal with anybody. But, what they don't know is that when somebody hurts them bad enough to do some good they won't feel as big as they do. They think that they are so grown that they don't need to go to school and learn. This is a poem about them.
You just going to waste your time,
trying to be fine.
Don't want to see yourself behind
when all your friends
are gone up in time.
You can't live all alone.
Got to find someone at home.
So you won't be left behind." (Laverta Jean)

*****

"Bring it out
Don't let it stay in
It been in too long." (Penny).

*****

"This person is a soft slightly individual. He is going right where he wants to go--nowhere. I've been a good friend of his now for many years. His character is really what you would call different, not bad mind you, just very different. His personality and character would take a stranger many years to figure out, to where he would accept him as a good person, rather than a quiet, paranoid, scared person. He's not really a smart or dumb person, but the way his mind, works when he's through with the world he'll have felt he's made it to his limit. He's the kind of person that would be happy with whatever he had, no matter how small.

What turns him off? I can hardly think of what turns him on. As far as I know everything turns him off. He has no smell, or nothing distinct about him except his paranoid vibes that most people get from him. I think he does most of his bleeding on the outside. He is incapable of hiding his emotions." (Miles).

*****

"Some of the boys at this school are very nice and they like to be called "young men" and some of them act like young gentlemen. But, the everyday boy just acts stupid and girlish. They are always talking about things that they don't even know. Like today when my cousin's dog followed me to school. She is a girl dog, about five or six months old and really fat. She was fat when they got her and the boys were saying that she was pregnant and she is really not, and anyway she has never been in heat.

Somebody or a man teacher ought to get all of the opposite sex that act like girls and have a real man to boy talk. When a girl's chest starts to develop they are all trying to make fun of them and I always tell them if they want a big chest to go and buy them some at a store and then they won't have to worry about girl's chests as they will have one of their own." (Puddingtang).

*****

"Pam is here
Pam is there
Pam really care." (Ella).

*****

"I think she feels pretty sure of herself. She is pretty much around people who think differently than herself but it doesn't change her ideas. She isn't very happy most of the time. She seems kind of frail and she is hurt very easily. The color of her feelings are a pale pink. I think she only puts on a small front. She acts like she's happy sometimes when I think she's sad because she doesn't want anyone to know. Her sound is a soft voice or a giggle now and then, otherwise silence. She is very lonely. The one word that describes her is "perfection." (Dusty).

*****

"Kimberly, Kimberly, why are you so cute? Are you really ever serious about the things you say and do?" (Edith).

*****

"Little Green Man what a girl
who would some day like to travel around the world
Sometimes happy never sad, A girl I thought was never bad
Little Green Man, no lost time here, Always smiling, never a tear." (Doris).

*****

"Well, now I'll tell you why I don't like Martha. Martha has always whined. Even since I first really knew her (in the seventh grade)I have known that. She would beg for part of your lunch and, after you give her something grudgingly, she spreads the thank-you and oh-your-sooo-nice so thick that its pitiful. She has always been loud and boisterous. This year she has taken yet another attitude which I find sickening. This time she has been hanging around with black kids (which I don't mind) but now she is trying to act like them, with the slang and voice and acting and its such a bad show that it makes me sick every time I'm near her. I know that the black don't particularly care for it either." (Edwina).

*****

"I would say this person is angry inside about one quarter of a day twice a week. Only major things make him real mad. This person tends to look up to himself as an idol. For the time I've known him in school he seems to brag at times usually when someone pays him a compliment." (Fritz the Cat).

*****

"People are funny. You can know someone for so long then they won't even talk to you anymore. It's not really funny, its sad. Its really sad that people think that little of others. The person I wrote this about really has fucked up his mind so much that he really couldn't care about someone if he wanted to. But I still love him." (Emily Marie).

*****

"Some boys I like, some I don't, some just bug the hell out of me. My little brother does some of that. He is always fighting and giving away his food. He is so give full. I hate boys that try to pimp too much and if they grow bumps all over their face I don't like them. I like black boys and white-boys. I like them by their action or intelligent looks." (Prudence).

*****

"Lonely
Is to be in a world
By yourself with
No one
Or no thing
In a dark
shadow of death
and humiliation
and aggravation
with no hesitation
she fills an inspiration
for a new world." (Roger).

*****

"A woman she is
So kind and free
She take me in
And she conforms me.
She has her life
That no one can change
She is free and bold
In such a beautiful way.
She sits by a shore
And waits for the dawn

So beautiful is she
May she never be gone.
She is so proud
Of what she is.
A swan she is
With her head held tall
And she is loved
By many a friend." (Janie).

*****

"The Bay is silent
There is no wind to wrinkle the water
The silence of the night
Gliding down to catch a
It breaks
Into a hundred ripples
It's white caps breaking
As they hit the beach
Silhouetting along the shore
Her hair blowing in the wind
As the water splashes upon her feet" (Emily Marie).

*****

"Black skin, liquid brown eyes, teeth, hair and nerve." (Adam).

*****

"Of green she sits
So quiet, so free
One day I shall go
And in peace shall be.
This place of green
Where dwarfs do sleep
And fish do swim
In the ocean deep.
(I don't think these are very good
but I think I'll turn them in anyway)." (Janie).

*****

"Nice and kind is what she is

Black and Proud is what she is pushing to be." (Love Bug).

*****

"This person can work in a somewhat talkative crowd. A lot of people can't do that but he has been able to get something done while talking. He can evaluate people. His evaluations, no matter how you feel about the other person, always have some sort of understanding or logic behind it. Not just a wild guess, but something that has some basis. He has a way of being able to talk to most people. He can talk to most anybody. One of his problems, not all the time but some of the time, is he like to tell someone to do this and not that and then he goes off and does what he told the person not to do.

    He is having a fight about himself. He seems to be fighting for something but he is not sure what. Like he has brought himself to believe that the country is run under capitalism. He knows it isn't true, but he just kept pounding it into himself until he does believe it. He hasn't quite found himself yet. The problem is he thinks he has found himself but he hasn't. I'm not really sure how he feels about himself. Thats the problem. You try and probe him and you think you know how he feels, and suddenly he does something that blows apart your whole theory. He is not really angry with himself. I think what turns him off about school is like this text. He doesn't mind describing somebody, he like that, but when you put these little stars and tell him to do this question, it won't work. If he has to do something like this he has to do it in his own way. When everybody is just stabbing around about what they want to say about a person, he can find it." (Xathier X. Zeus).

*****

"Some girls don't worry about some things and they should. Like dandruff, and the way they wear their clothes, and their hair. Some wear wigs and they think they look good but they look like hairy monster to me. I like girls that wear plain clothes and wear their hair plain. I don't like them girls that wear those fancy clothes." (Anon).

*****

"This person feels dissatisfied about herself. The one word that best describes them is "lonely." This person is unhappy inside. The color of her feeling are light green.

I think that life is not easy for this person. This person faces a lot of pressure at school, at home and within herself. She is worrying about keeping up her school work and being liked by other people, as well-liked as her friends are. She is not out-going or aggressive, but shy. This person is very sensitive." (New York, New York).

*****

"She do play a role. She acts like she is bad but really she isn't. She really is nice but she don't want people to know that she is nice and I don't know the reason why." (Tamila Shalon).

*****

"He's a mean little fucker. He's short and strong, if you're scared of him, he'll kick you around.
He's pushed me up, and he's pushed me down.
But he ain't gettin his fingers into my pocket.
He took Red Alex and made him stand,
Eyes closed and stiff, while he slapped his face.
I won't turn from that motherfucker,
An if he ever tries to take anything from me,
Scared as I am,
I'll fight till the blood flows free. (Adam).

*****

"I feel that it is very hard to express my feeling about this person because on the outside of it everything is alight but, deep inside, it really doesn't seem that way. To me the reason why the person acts that way is because there isn't enough attention toward that person. They don't really feel good about themself because it shows when they are dehumanized. The person smells like some bark in a tree.

I feel that the person does need a lot of comforting by the way the person acts. The person is always putting up a front when they are hurting. Inside I feel that they are afraid of defeat. I think that they are lonely inside." (Edward).

*****

"Lisa, Linda, Laura and Becky, here is four chicks, that has got their self together." (Puddingtang).

*****

"On the golden hills,
'Neath the purple haze,
Walks a beautiful maiden.
She is in a daze.
She walks through the trees, While her long robes flow, And the moon is high, Where ever she'll go.
And she sits by a lake,
And she dreams of times,
When life was easy,
And love was plentiful." (Janie).

*****

"Roses are red, violets are blue, but her favorite color is BLACK." (Francis).

*****

"She is far-outly
she is happy
she has many
friends and then she
doesn't, she loves, she hates, she cries, she laughs, she is lonely in a quiet way, not knowing herself why, she has lovely hair and beautiful eyes, she is Laural." (Emmy).

*****

"The shyest thing ah ever did see. But she is almost smarter than me. Some people do not know you can still be smart even if you learn slow." (Tony Jackson).

*****

"He is here, he is there, he is almost everywhere.
 he has his times, he has his poems,
 he has his mushrooms and his combs,
 he has his pot and smokes alot,
but he is real.
He has his fits, which are not too cool,
But I know not who has not at times.
He is there
He is Nathan." (Emmy).

*****

"He stands in a crowd
Not noticed at all
Once we all loved him
But now he's not there.
I think not of him
But of others I love
He stands all alone
With his chain in his hand." (Janie).

*****

"This person is shy and afraid to feel good about themselves. This person is modest on the outside, but maybe not when she's alone. The color of this person's feeling are green and blue for nature and the sky. Their smell is sweet, their feel is soft. They think mostly of Indians and cats." (Maria).

*****

"While the lily pads float
On the still water.
The moon shines through the clouds
To show the boy
Who sits by the pond.
He dreams of life
When there were no wars
When we lived
To love and be loved

He dreams of life
That will never come
This boy he goes to the
pond at night
To sit and dream
For love
The love he's never had
But hopes to get
From the pond
With the lily pads." (Janie).

*****

"Because I feel men are essentially made up of the same thing I feel they can easily trade places. You can trade places. You can trade places easily if the person is talking. For instance, if he talking about the Vietnam war I would say to myself, "What would I be thinking if I said that?

I feel this person thinks almost nothing of himself at the present, just what he is going to be in the future. This person has a paper route, not because he wants money now, but because he wants to be a doctor later. This person is also sort of quiet, but he isn't shy, he's thinking of the future. He isn't lonely, and he's not the sort of guy who will follow you around if you say hello to him. He likes school only because you have to be educated to be something later. This person feels nothing can happen to him now because his real life is in the future.

This person smells like he'll put his perfume on later, and he isn't finished painting his color yet. Its like when this person was born, he said, "I will work in the beginning of my life and become something later." Never taking into consideration that he might not make it. At the rate he's going now I think he'll make it easily." (Potassium Nacnud).

*****

"She would most like to be in a place where she could find something new out. A different country or culture. She is interested in things going on today and is very concerned. She would like to be something that is new and challenging. She is willing to try a new thing and is not afraid to be herself. She would most like to be with a person who could tell her something new and exciting. A revolutionary.

She is very creative and shows her imagination in her personality. Inside she is very thoughtful and quiet. She likes to be alone. She is very sure of herself but is troubled by the world and her problems." (Vouix).

*****

"There is really no words for
his description.
Nothing but WOW!" (Puddingtang).

*****

"One day I was sitting with George. George took my pieces of paper and trouk them up. I mean he messed them up. That bad nigger makes me sick most of the time. He look like a big black bear.

One day he went up in the woods took off his clothes and ran all around Marin City trying to pee on everybody. If you ever see him this is how he looks. Big black green teeth, gold eyes, mucky hands, red lips and hair that looks like sheep shit." (Bettina).

*****

"Someone has to bring this student out of his fear. His feelings stay black all the time from being pushed aside. His world is also blue from crying.

You who are scared, You who are frightened, come into the world and watch it lighted. For good things are to come." (Somon Marie).

*****

"Dear Friend,
I like you but sometimes you are a little of you know what. I mean by a little be of crazy. Sometimes you get on my nerves. Like always hitting on me and messing with me all the time, and

laughing, and sucking on the pencil eraser, and being so nosey, and looking so crazy all the time, and staring at people all the time, and liking boys, and sitting around at lunch-time looking sad and fussing with people.

    I still remember that time you came to school with two stitches in your face looking like a scared rabbit from nowhere. And thats all." (Edith).

*****

"As she walks along the floors of sand.
Her blonde hair blows in the wind.
The gulls fly high above
The ocean roars.
She falls to her knees
Then she falls to the ground
For death has struck
And the sun has set." (Janie).

*****

"A Friendship:
A friend called
and asked why I didn't like her
I said I was eating
couldn't talk
would call later
I called
talked
I said that a long time ago
I loved the way she was
That she loved life
and believed in what she
believed in
But now she didn't care
and not caring is something
that hurts
Hurts harder than opposition

I said it hurts
and I don't want to be around her then
As cold as she could
she said
Thank you for telling me
And hung up." (Adam).

*****

"Harry Simpson is a right-on blood.
Harry Simpson never wears them floods.
Harry Simpson is never sloppy.
Harry Simpson has no hobby.
Harry Simpson is not very mean.
Harry Simpson is always clean.
Harry Simpson is always sharp.
Harry Simpson I think is smart.
Now Harry Simpson knows where its at.
Now can you argue with that?" (Tony Jackson).

*****

"Did you ever realize that there are a lot of weird people in this class? I'm just looking at everybody and people are kind of weird looking. Especially fingers and toes. Fingers are five long skinny things coining out of a short fat thing. Fingers bug me. If I run my other fingers down them they give me the creeps. You can feel the bones and all that. And when you think about it what are they like inside? All bloody and nerves and gristle. Toes are ugly. They look like five square things coming out of a fat square thing.

Have you ever looked at everybody when they are still and looked at all the weird faces and positions they are in? Are you studying to become a psychologist and is that why you want these dumb pages?

I never know what to write about. Most of the weird people don't go here anymore. Last year there was this girl and me and her would walk around like cats and talk baby talk. In the fourth grade there was more weird people. We would go into hysterics anytime someone would mention a hippopotamus or a rhinoceros.

Did you notice all the giggly people in this class? This person sitting next to me started giggling because you fell in a desk. Why do boys like to tease girls by putting their arm around them or saying something? Never mind, don't answer that. I know they're just weird like everybody else." (Valerie Valias).

*****

"I think this person would most like to be with other people and at parties. She makes friends (or at least tries) with everybody. I'm a very good friend of Her's. We share problems and work them out together.

She would most like to be doing her own thing with her own man like I do. She would most like to be with talkative people because she talks a lot herself. She is lovable, friendly, talkative and very playful. She doesn't have anything against people who are not her color. She makes friends with everyone, even the one's who talk behind her back and then talk sweet to her in front of her face. Those people (most of them) are her own color.

I think she feels right-on with herself. Her smell is sharp. Her feeling are soft. She's very tender-hearted and gets heart broken easily. So do I." (Lynn).

*****

"She is wonderful
she is happy
she has strange moods. She is up and down and all around she needs love,
and lacks a lot, for what she's got is not the same. I think by now you've guessed her name, she is a friend. I love her dearly she is my friend she is real, she is Sonia." (Emmy).

*****

"He feels good inside and he is fairly secure with himself. He is not angry with himself. He is very imaginative. Personally I don't think he needs comforting. As I said, he is a secure person.

He puts up a front sometimes. Like he talks about how much black people are suppressed but he really doesn't have any black friends. He stays in a white bag. He is a happy person inside and is a little afraid of what the world might come out to be. Like Destruction I mean. Towards different people he has different feelings. Like people who are his friends and people active in the things he does, the colors would be red or orange. People who are preaching war and messing with black people and are just mainly racists, the color would be black or gray.

He mainly thinks of world problems, like suppression and racialism. The word that describes him is "active." (Ian).

*****

"To me some boys are nice, but some think they are too good to be true. I do not have nothing against boys, but some boys wear their pants too tight, and some of them try and swish when they walk. Some boys are so ugly that they could scare you with one look. Now their hair. Some boys do not comb their hair for weeks, some wear their hair long and sometimes it looks good, but if it is too long, it has got to go. And I hate boys with rollers in their hair." (Penny).

*****

"Friends:
Friends, friends, friends. Do you think you've got any?
I would say: I don't know.
One minute they say you're their friend, the other, the opposite.
What should I do, go out and buy friends, no, no, I can't.
Remember what I said." (Jake Brown).

*****

Johnny is a young man
Johnny is black
Johnny is a good dresser
Now how about that
He never throws food away
Unless it is not good

His favorite is salami
He'd eat a horse if he could.
Don't get me wrong
He can sing a song
But if you listen
You'll soon be gone." (Tony Jackson).

*****

"George is black, George is fat, George is ugly, but George is cool." (Francis).

*****

"He thinks he's great, he thinks he is smart, when he knows that he's not. He seems to be friendly, sometimes meanly. He likes the sweet smell, the sour smell, the drug smell as well. He feels hard and rough. Hardly needs comfort, always playing a part. His mind is sex, sex, drugs, drugs, sex, drugs.

Sight, hearing, speech, touch, it makes no difference. He seems to be a nut, acting like a nut, sounding stupid and mentally ill, looking like an accident going somewhere to happen. Looking stupid, lonely and hopeless, worrying about the future." (Pimpy).

*****

"I have a feeling that someday all my friends will really be my friends, not pushy people that play games, but people I can trust, people that I can have respect for and who will give me respect.

I was once in love, but no sir, that's not for me. I think I'll just be a rambler, never settle down, just travel around awhile." (Suzi Mantele).

*****

"Memories of being loved
Comes back to find a few
That love her again
Falls back into herself
Shows no feelings
She becomes a shy, quiet nobody
Comes to school only to see People.

I think she is somewhat like the man in, "A Most Peculiar Man". I think that if she died people would say, "What a shame that she's dead, but wasn't she a most peculiar girl." She is really very pretty and I don't see why she isn't popular. I think she feels pretty good about herself but is bewildered about why not very many other people like her." (Janie).

*****

"There is this girl that I know that is really a female dog (bitch) and she thinks she is the greatest thing on earth like she's god's gracious gift to the human race and someday I am going to pick a fight with her and knock all her teeth out cause there's a deep down right hatred I've developed for her when I get ahold of her. I'll kill-her with my bare hands." (Suzi Mantele).

*****

"The sun is shining and there's plenty of light since I lost my baby. The sun has been bright since I lost my baby. The beautiful spring days have turned into cold winter nights." (Roger).

*****

"Friends:
Friends are love, friends are joy,
friends are trust, friends are harmony,
friends are unhappy, friends are presumptuous,
friends are real, friends are here,
friends are beautiful, friends are hope,
friends are something you feel in your heart,
friends are life." (Emmy).

****

16. More "Tupages."

As weeks went by, an increasing number of students used the opportunity to express themselves.

"Life is a dream
We are living in a dream
But most of the time it is
A nightmare.
A nightmare with wars
Wars that never end but go on and on killing more people every second." (Emily Marie).

*****

"Your Songs
What do smoking give
You do it make you feel like a grown up or even like your father
No it make you feel big; do it make you feel good; no not after a good while. I'd bet it don't Make you feel as good as kissing a lady's hand.

You could pull a girl's hair rather than smoke it don't seem hard to begin smoking, but to start smoking and don't never stop it is hard very hard and ugly, do you want your songs or not." (Jake Brown).

*****

"An Uninspired Poem.
Sunlight shines through the room window,
Lighting colors in the room.
Colors of nature.
Living cells--with a history, a past.
You people with a future.
What of it?" (Eleanor Hume).

*****

"Life is going through things you never went through before. Discovering the new and the old, life and death, love, hatred.

Kindness means wisdom, knowledge that no books ever had been written in this time or date.

For life is from heaven not hell." (Roger).

*****

"The sky the earth the stars above
Will ring out loud about brotherly love.
The wind the sun the birds the bees
Will ring it out loud through the trees.
The moon the mountains the ocean and man
Will know of happiness throughout the land.
When the sun sets low
The earth's song mellows gently
And the moon brings love.
I wonder what this world would be
Without all the other people like me.
Do you think that there is a God?
I've thought about it sometimes but that is a
Question that I don't think anyone can answer
And be sure.
Tomorrow I think I will buy
Some different colored popcorn. Won't that be a gas?" (Suzi Mantele).

*****

"What is life to me? It's wishing and "looking forward" and dreaming. For most people its money, to cheat people to make money, to get bribed for money, people get mean for money. In the city people shove and push their own kind, they show hate, be bitchy. People get jobs they don't like but to make money. I think we're getting over crowded. In order to get away you have to have money, so people get mad when they are crowed, when they make money. As for me do I like money? Of course, but all through my life, when I make money, I'm not going to cheat, bribe, or steal for money just to satisfy me. Because I'm hurting them, and when I hurt them I get hurt just as much. This probably makes your head go round to read this paper but I think it's true.

I'm going to make a promise to myself that when I grow up I'm not going to get tired very easily. I want to stay healthy and stay running instead of sitting on my butt all day and worrying about dying (like some people). I'm going to trust people, have fun and live and never, never die.

Oh yea, I hope my skin doesn't get wrinkled and my veins don't show. I don't want to get old! Who doesn't? I worry too much, but not that much. I just thought about this and wrote it down."
(Rabbit Paranoia)

*****

"What is Truth people ask.
Is it telling no lies?
Yes it is,
But it is not told.
Today children are told war is good.
The war is the only way in the world
To solve problems of today.
Some children of today are told
Stay away from the black person,
They will harm you in many ways.
Children of today are told many lies.
Children of tomorrow might know the truth,
But today truth hasn't been told.
When will truth be realized?" (Kat Hart).

*****

"Sex is wonderful. Sex is good. No one can tell me different. I like sex and the girls too because James Brown made a record called "It's a Man's World." It is a woman's world. God made us to have sex and I am glad of that. If it is a man's world man can not make sex with another man and have a baby. And a man can not make another man feel good. So it is not a man's world, it's a woman's world.

True women will get you into trouble, but if I loved a woman she can get me into trouble but I will have sex with her and then she better not say anything about it. If she does I will beat her and that will be putting force on her and she will have to take the force and be glad with it.

So sex is not a bad thing for some people because all people do not think the same. But some people think the same and some one thing like I am because that person like sex is good and if it was no sex it will not be people in this world today so because there are sex people is enjoying it and I have done sex with a girl and it made me feel good and I guess she was feeling good and as long as I live I will get sex from more than one girl some people may not like sex but the ones that like sex I am happy for them because they have good feeling about sex." (Chuck).

*****

"a broken tree
a broken pencil
a mind.
a broken earth
a broken car
a broken plane
a broken hand
a broken air
a war
a mended tree
a mended pencil
a mended mind
a mended earth
a mended car
a mended plane
a mended hand
a mended air
a mended war
a life blossoms." (Rabbit Paranoia).

*****

"The following is a list of all the bad things I can think of: water pollution, air pollution, land pollution, lying, cheating, shooting, knifing, tripping, pushing, killing, poverty, capitalism, prejudice, Spiro Agnew, money, speed, addiction, race riots, greed, bullets, the A-bomb, cars, the destruction of plants, over-population, death, suspicion, illiteracy, some drug laws, planes, opium, murder, time, wars, slanted reporting, Richard Nixon, generation gap, alcohol, the moon landings, big business, the United States, missiles, the H-bomb, oppression, the death of wildlife, the growth of cities, the government, birth, grades, national guard, violence, marriage, space, and many, many others." (Simon).

*****

"What is knowledge? Is knowledge knowing how to make a bomb or knowing how to make money? Is it examining your experiences from some drug? Is it discovering yourself or making love? Is it real? Will anything I "learn" count? Is asking questions learning? Is finding the answers learning? What isn't knowledge? What isn't learning?" (Adam).

*****

"Apollo 13 was a moon shot that didn't reach the moon. In fact it just barely got back to the earth. Something went wrong on the craft. An explosion took place and the result was no air. The Apollo 13 crew had just enough air to last them on the trip back to earth. The astronauts barely escaped death, and now the astronauts want to go back. Call it brave if you want to. It's pure dumbness to me. But that's how my brain thinks. Ain't no way in the world that I am going to do something I almost lost my life on once. No buddy, life is too important for that." (Tony Jackson).

*****

"You have 71 days left to prepare yourself for high school and the rest of your life". Life is sad, happy, you name it. It goes on with many happenings which cannot be described. Life is a goal. A goal to be fulfilled. Life is dreaming, looking, feeling, reaching out for what is there. I don't know life at all. Life is different to many people, that is why people don't get along. There is yesterday, today and tomorrow... forever more." (Rabbit Paranoia).

*****

"I was talking to someone the other day who said that no matter what we do it doesn't matter, that everything is trivial. I told him to go back to bed. If it doesn't matter, if its all too trivial, then life is worthless, and I have yet to hear of anything that nature (or God) has made that is worthless. Life maybe is a colossal accident but it certainly did something to the state of this earth. If life is an accident maybe we should destroy it. I'm not sure we can. Certain insects and other low forms of life can adapt very quickly to pollution. Probably they could adapt to radiation. I doubt if it is an accident. Who could make a mistake like that?" (Washington Irving).

*****

"As I walk these lonely streets I think and dream what life's about. I wonder why this life's so hard, why the birds are able to fly and why everything is moving so fast. It seems like only yesterday was the past, for now I think it's all a dream, and hope I never awaken to it's horrible reality. That's what we live in. Although this world is beautiful you know. So many times you see this planet as the most wonderful thing in the universe." (Emmy).

*****

"I'm thinking of moving to Canada or a socialist country. I like the idea of moving to a socialist country. I'm not scared to learn a new language. I am scared to learn a new culture. I don't want to leave my friends, or the climate, or the countryside, or some of the fights that are going on. If I'm going to leave this country I'd rather leave now than later because I'll have more time to adjust, and more time to live with whatever things I'll have. I'll have more time to make new friends. It seems like running out. I'll have to think about it. I'm not doing anything here so maybe leaving isn't so bad." (Washington Irving)

*****

"I just found out when we die we're going to fertilize the soil and feed the birds. That sort of makes me feel better about dying because we'll be at least repaying the life that is left (if any) and the earth; which is something we surely haven't been doing." (Rabbit Paranoia).

*****

"Somewhere there lies truth
Somewhere the truth will open
The ugly will unfold
And the forgotten truth will soon return
And be reality
There can be love
Love is so good
Hope is coming
And joy will spread
But where oh where
Somewhere." (Emmy).

*****

"To me life is love, you have to love somebody to live. Without love you're nothing but a thing, worthless, useless and forgotten. Life is a temptation. Everybody want to live always and it's not possible. Life is sometimes mean, soft, sweet, hard and also dreadful. Nobody can live a lifetime without being hurt." (B. J.).

*****

"I don't want to die
In high school
I don't want to get run
from that car
I don't want to die
In bed
I don't want to die
In an airplane
I want to die

On a mountain
In a field
In the ocean
A long time from now
A longer way from home." (Adam).
*****

"Its a righteous day, And the flowers are poppin
And there's work to be done, And words to be written
And money to be spent
Oh, yes forget that--Money to be "spent"
When you got a lid, You got new friends." (Adam).
*****

"There is a place beyond the sun
That has been there every since the world begun
When a person dies, or is born, A little piece of this place is torn
A song comes out of the tear
Begging all on earth not to despair." (Suzi Mantele).
*****

"Love of who? Love of what? Happiness how?
Can you love something you don't understand?
Is understanding peace of mind?
Can happiness derive from sin?
Love, Peace, and Happiness,
As everyone say
But I can't wait
Until that day,
Which I know will never come in anyway." (Doris).
****

17. Assignment: The Robot Computer

An illuminating episode for me was the case of the "robot computer." One day, while driving home from school, I saw a dressmaker's dummy that had been left on a corner. Its humanoid form gave me an idea, so I took it home.

Fitted with a plastic jug and a couple of red light bulbs for the head and eyes, some dangling wires, and sprayed silver, with lots of imagination, it could pass as a robot.

After being wheeled into the room, the thing told the class, via a concealed tape recorder, that it was part of a computer that could answer any question fed into it.

The students were given stacks of I.B.M. cards and asked to write their questions on the cards and put them into a slot on robot's chest. They were told, however, that to operate a computer is extremely expensive and therefore they should ask only those questions that were really important to them.

They could ask as many questions as they liked, and the questions could be anonymous.

Initially, I had planned this activity to be an introduction to a unit on data processing and statistics, which would conclude with a visit to an office compute installation so they could see how the system worked.

Also, I thought that we could figure out answers for many of the questions; quoting statistical probabilities for such questions as, "How long will I live? or "How much money will I make?

Thinking the class would take the robot as a joke, I was not prepared for the fact that students would take the assignment seriously. Many of them really believed that the robot was capable of doing all I said, and asked questions of deep personal significance.

Six hundred and twenty-two questions were asked. Many were quite commonplace and to be expected: "When will I die?" (51), "Will I go to college?" (47), "What sort of job will I have?" (41),

"What's going to happen in the future?" (19), "Will I have money?" (19).

Thirteen questions were on drugs. In this group three asked why people take drugs, five asked if drugs are as harmful as people say. One, signed "Stoned" asked, "Am I going to be a speed freak or a drug addict?" while another wrote, "I've been hooked once, will I be hooked again?"

A group (73), focused on war and pollution. "When will the war end?" "Will smog kill everybody before the year 2000?" "Will I ever have to go to Vietnam?" "Is this sick society going to get any sicker?"

The most interesting questions were those concerning personal problems (133). Some of these were quite ordinary, such as, "Will I get some new books?", while fifty-three cards asked about personal relationships, (mostly asking whether or not the questioner was liked by his peers).

Forty-three of the cards (and one must remember this was group of seventy-five students at most) inquired about really personal problems. I found those most poignant. Here is a selection:

Six questions were on religion, (e.g., "Will I go to heaven?", "Is immaculate conception possible?") and six on race, ("How did people get their colors?").

Love, sex and marriage was a big topic (133). This group of questions was mostly concerned with: "Who will I marry?" (35), "Does X really love me?" (19), "How many kids will I have?" (26), and "Am I going to have a baby before I get out of high school?" or "Will I get pregnant soon?" One card asked, "Am I pregnant?"

Others asked:
"Why am I so mean?"
"When will I become of normal size?"
"Does anyone like me?"
"Will mother break her bad habits?"

"Am I going to stop stuttering?"
"When will my mother come back home?"
(and, in the same handwriting)
"Will I ever see my father?"
"Is my father really sicker than he acts?"
"I want to destroy. Can you tell?"
Most poignant was, "Is my mother really dead or is she only sleeping?"

****

These then, are the thoughts weighing on the minds students, while I am muttering on about the "separation of powers," or the "Continental Congress."

18. Assignment: Mr. Aston's Mid-Year Report

As you know, at this school we don't give grades, only comments. Write a mid-year report on me.

"I think that you're about the best teacher that I have and I'm not even trying to get better grades from you." (Lief Erickson).

*****

"Mr. Aston, I am superbly, pissed off at you for telling me to shut up when I got up to sharpen my pencil. I think it was a superbly stupid thing to do.

You're getting more like Mrs. Hinton. Do this, do that. Bitch, bitch, bitch at us all about some irrelevant thing that nobody could give a damn about anyway.

You probably think that this little paper has an over abundance of cuss words. I am using them to get across a point and they match my mood.

The main reason I wrote this though was because I am so damn, disappointed that you were so mad about something that you had to yell at me.

If you can't find anything better to do than that I advise you to go jump off a certain span that connects San Francisco to Marin County." (Harry Bippo).

*****

"My friends and I have noticed how shy you are when you get up in front of the class. You get up and scratch your head, smile and look at the floor and then you put your right hand in your pocket. Do you feel insecure in front of us or in front of 8th graders? I have many things, hold it, not many but a few things to talk about. First of all, things which bother or should I say bug the shit out of me, are things like that day you asked about my Wednesday cutting of school. First of all, I had never left school that day during schooltime. I had only gone down to the end of the asphalt path and sat on the white fence (note: which is on the school grounds) and I never went further than there. What I think happened was a Mother Fucking Pig of a teacher saw me sitting there and somehow this asshole concocted that pile of bullshit saying that I was out. I think Ass'es like this should keep their mouths shut until they positively know what they are talking about. Another thing which angers me is, that when that first seagull was hit with rocks I got the blame, and if looks could kill I would have been dead a long time ago. Then, when the second one was hit, it was Joe and them who killed it, both times I had never thrown rocks all day. Some people are really fucked those who hit the seagulls and those who blame the innocent ." (Joe Fork).

*****

"I am finding out that you are a good teacher because you let any student come in during recess, playing records, dance, and talk. When you go out of the room you let us stay in instead of making us go out of the room like any other teacher would. You hold someone responsible until you come back from where you were. When group 12 is in your class you want them in the class on time and sit down and get the work and ask questions if they need help. When the class gets going good people start getting out of their seats and talking. I don't think you see what is going on in the class really. I think you trust the black students that come in a recess because you let them stay there by themselves with important things around the room like money, grade book and maybe other things around important in the class." (Prudence).

*****

"Mr. Aston has a way of keeping a very relaxed atmosphere in the classroom. A good sense of humor, a long temper, patience and understanding. All these things make a great teacher, Mr. Aston has them all. As long as its not disturbing the rest of the class you can do anything you want as long as you make sure your assignments get in on time. He treats everyone the same. He listens to whatever you say to him and if you make a joke if he thinks its funny he'll laugh." (Sir Genius).

*****

"Mr. Aston some of the kids things you are shity but to me you are a good man. Some of the kids they hell at you and do some more things beside that. And I see why you say shit and some more thing and when we go to the asemle [student government assembly] and some of the kids say one thing bad a about you and the next thing you all the kids in the asmele join the once that said that firh thing about you and they call you nambs the firch time you cum her you did not gave the kids a inuft time to get good with you and you did not geve them a inuft time-but to me you are good to group 12 but some of the kids do not truy you right but to me I do and you trey me right." (Chuck).

*****

"Mr. Aston, this is what I think of you. I think you are going the wrong way by giving too much homework and using the word "hell." I think you want to do things your way and no one elses way. I don't think you could sit down and have a discussion on something without getting mad and probably cussing. I think you put on a front sometimes just to get people mad." (Hugh).

*****

"Well right now I'm thinking about how mad you make me. Every time I say something it seems that you turn it around to suit you. And the way you got mad at me this morning. Why? Because I was reading another book. Oh, sometimes you make me sick. I'm so tired of having people get mad at each other. I'm sick of you and your stupid class. I'm so mad at you I could scream! You better not say anything to me. Because, if you do, I'll really get mad inside of me and who knows what might happen. So I think you'd better mind your own business. Anyway, I think you're prejudiced against girls." (Wildflower Weed).

*****

"Shit'n and Bitch'n: You say you are tired of everybody saying shit and bitching when you give them assignments. Well, it just so happens that I don't believe I have ever bitched or said shit when you have given assignments. You should get your problems out on the people that do bitch and say shit to your assignments. Mr. Aston, did you write "manure" on the board cause you thought that someone was going to put "shit" on their paper? Mr. Aston you shouldn't be afraid. The world can't' hurt you and if you crawl back into your shell then it won't settle your problem. By the way, where are all the kids in our class? For instance where is Clayton? Why don't you keep track of your students? You are always complaining about low attendance." (Suzi Mantele).

*****

"You have a hang-up just like anyone else. You take your problems out on us. Take this morning for instance, you came on foul, saying that you had drunk champagne last night and had a hangover. That's not our problem. You don't realize that man can't go on through life the way he has been doing. I realize that as a person you must do your thing, just like anybody else, but not in the way that you do it though. I have problems just like anybody else. I also must cope with them. To prepare myself for high school and the rest of my life I must face life as it is. And so must you." (Somon Marie).

*****

"Aston is high, Aston is low, Aston is around, Aston is down, Aston is up, But he is cool." (Francis).

*****

"Hello Mr. Aston, how are you? Do you slouch because you are so tall or do you slouch because you just have not learned to stand up straight." (Washington Irving).

*****

"To me sometimes you're a flower and sometimes you're just dead weeds." (Shirley).

****

9. "The Mind is a Miracle."

Someone said "The Mind is a Miracle, what are your thoughts? Whether "far out," or offensive, these pages are worth recording as they show children testing the limits of creativity, as well as propriety.

"The Mind"

The mind is a miracle which no one can explore but yourself.

Night settles quietly upon us. The rain softly touches ground and rolls away. A mist touches moonbeams and dissolves them into blackness. The night is deep, untouchable.

Silent footsteps splash water on a sunken sidewalk. Rain trickles down the windows, blurring images of moonlit clouds. Damp air touches everything. The feel and sound of night in enveloping.

Fog settles upon a disappearing streetlight. Darkness clutches an old tree. A hill's outline is gone, night has captured it. Leaves rustle faintly as the night settles quietly upon us." (Vouix).

*****

"One hand clapping is the pebble
that starts the avalanche,
the first man
in a revolution." (Adam)

*****

"Taylor Park
The sunlight water gleaming
sizzles through the forest green light stream of the green pastures
while footsteps lashed brushing dirty muddy water in our faces
that knocked us back in our places
The enchanted forest
Out in wilderness
of the shadow of Jerusalem
in the golden suspense of pleasure
on life's merry-go-round

Respect one another white or black in the enchanting forest above where suspense of the golden forest sky a fire burns enchanting glow of redwood" (Roger).

*****

"Freedom in the sky
Is the birds that fly so high
On wind currents
They do their feats
With curved wings and bent tails,
They glide along,
Along the paths
That currents make.
They're like the fish
In the ocean.
They're separate,
But together.
In flocks
and schools
They all go on their own,
But their own is with others." (Mark).

*****

"Ho hum, ta da. Here comes the Iguana man walking down the street. Clip clop, says the barber as he shaves the head of an anvil. Locker chairs running around the room in undivided attention to the wall as they spin the electric rotators in direction not pertaining to the current state of affairs.

    Earrings on the head of nails. Nose-clips for sale. Fifty-cents for orange juice and cookies as well as the train set.

Blue coat, red coat, the British are coming if the yo-yo can free itself from the chair of injustice. Guns, bombs, war, peace, tranquility, love, do the scene of people skipping down the hill at a mild pace according to their strengths and weaknesses. Light shows going on and off that nobody seems to notice. Music playing as people play chess and checkers.

Mothers pray for their sons to come back from the war as visions of mattresses, wine, milk and honey float gently across the air. Green boards, chalk dust, electric sockets and impressions.

Bonnie and Clyde sit in the corner weaving bonnets for their mother-in-law and auntie. Robots with orange eyes roll slowly across the slightly tilted floor and dogs and cats shake hands after completing the assignment given them by the head owl of the forest of green and blue. Day dreaming images fly past as the shooting gallery and pinball machines ring out loudly. This is Strawberry Fields where nothing is real. Continuing with the tour of the magic forests of apples, oranges....[And so on for another three pages.]." (Harry Bippo).

*****

"Some Sayings:
Honky, nigger, faggot, cow,
cracker, peckerwood, Mr. Charlie.
Bitch, whore, bastard,
two bit dusty butt.
Creep, slew foot, Uncle Tom,
Jim Crow.
That is all I can think of right now
and don't get mad about all
of the dirty things on this paper." (Puddingtang).

*****

"I lie on the rocks like a devil, And think of the hate and good
And the pain and the blood, and the blood on the rocks,
and the blood in the sea, the blood from my heart
O the blood in the poison
The circles of blood, The circles of pain, as I lie on the rocks like Satan
Oh, the hate in the blood, and the pain in the hate
The weight of wrong, The weight of right
If it were just good, and just evil....
But its blood and pain, and circles of knowledge

And the sea goes out, and the sea comes it
and the waves are always new, and they always return
And there are circles of life, and blood and life in blood
and hate in blood
Is there love and hate, or is it another circle of blood
as I lie upon the rocks, like the devil
I think of sand, which springs from dying rocks
Oh sand, you are different with each grain
Blood, sea, sand, circles
And I lie on the rocks and the blood of my thoughts falls, and drips upon these rocks like the devil
And, as the blood of my thoughts spills out upon these rocks, Good and evil are so close they're not separate
So god and satan are one and the same,
 for there is no good without evil
As hate is born out of love can love be born out of hate, so I lie upon these rocks which are my mind and I cannot compare myself to Satan for Satan is the Lord and I cannot compare myself with God."
(Adam)

*****

"(This script is X rated)
"Who do you think you are?"
"God."
"God of what, your toes?"
"No, of God?"
"Why are you in this classroom?"
"Because -----"
"Do not use the Lord's name in vain!"
"All right then you mother----screwdriver!"
"How is the---- did a screwdriver get into
this, God dammit?"
"What did you want me to call you, Gratcho Marx or something?"
"That's Groucho Marx, O young one."
"Well answer my question, you nincompoop!"

"Which one? You must have many questions, O young one.
"Are you a fucker?"
"A what?"
"A fucker. You know, something like that thing sitting to the left of me."
"You mean me?"
"No, the Hunch-back of Notre Dame. Ha, ha, ha."'
"Enough of these sour-rank-old-mothers-of-a-question, ask me a real good one."
"Are you a sour-rank-old-mother-of-a-question?"
"That a boy! Its good to know you have an unsurpassed imagination and can actually ask me a question that has absolutely no connection with the first one."
"What a dumb fuck."
"A stupid sexual intercourse, to put it in real words."
"You mean me?"
"No, the Hunch-back of Notre Dame, ha, ha, ha. (Real imagination. I changed a period into a comma.)
"Oh shut hell up!"
"God has been trying to do that for years!"
"I knew that bastard couldn't do anything right."
"Such obscene language for one so young. The thought of it pains me. Merciful Heavens!"
"You dirty old man."
"Right on!"
"Right off!"
"Right in!"
"Right out!"
"Right up and down!"
"Right fuck!"
"No, wrong fuck! You got a boy, ha, ha, ha."
"Very unfunny."
"Very unimaginative. Very unprovocative.

But you aren't old enough for Granny Goose.   Hak, hak, ha."
"Provocative pervert!"
"Touche1" or "touchy."
"You bastard."
"What are you, the Frito Bandito or something?"
"Sheeet up!"
"Oh, you mean Sidhu."
"Shit no!"
"Fuck it man. Want to ball a chick?"
"Find a baby chicken that can play
ball and I'11 ball it!"
"What a horny ass-bastard. How horny can you get.
You ought to be castrated for life."
"What does "catastraped" mean?"
"You can't even spell it. I'm going to chop off your
balls so you won't be able to ball any baby chickens."
"Oh, boy!"
"Slit, chop, hack, blood, mmm, taste good!
Zap Comix forever!"
"Oh, boy. Eayaeeooop, Grunt, slit."
You really are a horny ass bastard.
"A what?"
"A reincarnation of Donald John Duncan!"
"The third, don't forget the third!"
"I don't see what you're worried about. Calling you
Donald John Duncan and including the 3rd is no compliment."
"Bastard."
"If you had said 'You bastard' we could of wrote the
same thing you said before."
"You're a bastard just the same!"
"I thought I was a bastard shit?"
(If you crumple the sheet once more, as you said,
I'll castrate you again.)
"Fuck you."

145

"I don't really want to trip."
"Faggot, faggot!" (Xathier X. Zeus).

*****

"Black is the night so heavenly light if there is truth Lord let us unite
Someday judgement day will come they are praying and saying when judgement day comes we will be destroyed by firey tongues when Jesus comes
Your eyes
can see
the beautiful
scenery across the seven seas and seven mountains of love, peace, freedom prosperity and let life shine it's bright guiding light for all
I can say must
be right for I will
find that golden light." (Roger)

*****

"Circle Games:
On and on and on. Round and round and circle in circle in circle rotating, with, against, with, against, with, against, with, against and clockwise and counter-clockwise, and clockwise and counter-clockwise, over and over and over and change and repetition and change and again, repetition, revolution, evolution, evolution, revolution. Change without change, change that's new, change that's old. Change that never changed. Revolution: change with violence--fast. Evolution: change without violence--slow." (Adam).

*****

"The world is in good shape. I've seen pictures. Its round and it has big blue things and little strips of white and gray dots. Its beautiful until you see it close up.

    I can just see every reason for the Apollo astronauts not to come back!
    Mission Control: "O.K., good show, come on back."
    Astronauts: "Chuck you , Farley, Send up some more air and beer please. Stop by if you want. Out."

Nice thoughts, huh? Will...
Excuse us, Sir, FBI. We have reason to believe that
you are talking like a Commie. STOP IT OR ELSE !"
"Yes sir. I'll stop soon, really, but please get off of my head, it hurts muchley much."
"O.K., but shape up or get shipped in."
"Good-bye." This has been a message from your local FBI. And don't play God anymore." (Anon).

*****

"Music:
Music entertains lots of people, lets say the majority of. the people on earth.
Music helps some people to think and remember things.
Music is the life of most people.
Music is like a big helping hand to some people.
Some people cannot work without having some music.
Music is like candy apples to some people, to others not in the least.
Some people are so simple that music don't attract their attention.
Some people cannot stand the screeching of loud music.
Some people like soft music, some don't, some like loud music, some like walzing music which is not too loud.
Music can be boring, that is sometimes, because they hear the same thing over and over, which is not too good.
Music starts from school where some people are in the school band.
Some people start liking music from the time they are about eight years old.
Music helps to make some people sleep at night when they are tired or worried.
Music is like a castle of wonders.
Music is the feeling of yesterday.
Music is happiness.
Music is thinking.
Music is looks.

Music is Nature.
Music is me
and you talking." (Jake Brown).

*****

"I just got back from somewheres I don't want to write about directly. But, an eternity is the time it takes for one object to meet another. Can you imagine how many eternities it takes for matter to reach anti-matter.

Picture yourself in the fetus position, spinning completely separate from anything. Now, since you're completely separate from everything your physical body is far, far behind. Each cell must be separate too.

Now, nothing is real or connected everything is simple all of the physical world is behind you spinning cells. Completely free. Can you imagine how long it will take to form a thought? Since everything is separate how can it unite? Soar above, so you don't worry about all that physical shit. It is so unimportant. Ah, how can you explain the unexplainable." (Adam).

*****

"Silver thistles cascade down an edge of the tree. Tumble on to infinity, soft as slate. Crash down into the slits of a comb to smash wet cotton. A convulsion removes objects to a further cove of bone, stung with honey and filled with wet cream. I'm hungry.

Pumpkin pie. Smooth golden crust to melt down your throat. Spoon it in and slather it all over your tongue. The texture is utterly good.

Strawberry shortcake. Mounds of strawberries drip out of the sides, out into the juice flows the cake. Sweetness and berries melting teeth to trickle past tonsils and linger for an instant on tongue.

Crunch. The chocolate candy melts and chewy delicious caramel evokes and smells to your nose. Mmm, it is so good to make me dizzy. Hot in here.

Piercingly, the noise stopped. Dead silence awoke the sleeping clock to a dull tick. Air rolled into balls and fell into corners, making the room foggy. The sky blurred, sharpened as the point of a thistle broke it. The hardened crust broke and through a small hole liquid sky flowed.

Thick blue streams fell and melted into mist. The dripping stopped and an unbearable noise put the clock to sleep and all was still." (Vouix).

*****

"Time-what is time? Is it a thing? Is it hard, is it soft? Is it real? Is it a dimension? The 1st? The 2nd? The 3rd? The 4th?

How many dimensions are there? 1? 2? 3? 4? 5? 6? 7?... ....What are the dimensions? Height, weight, depth, time? Do I know this for a fact? Is there anything I know that I was not taught?

What is smartness? What is I.Q.? Is it just a better remembrance of facts previously learned.

Who exists? Do I exist? Does a person still exist when I don't see them?

Time-does it have a sound? Does it have a color? Man has many sounds for time: tick-tick, tick-tock, bong, boooonnngggggg, ding, ding, ding, oh, oh, oh, wooooooooooo." (Simon.

*****

"Rain
Silvery spider, Trickle across heavy skies, Drooping forever.
Fog, Wispy curls of white, Encircle sloping mountains
Hiding their beauty.
High on a hilltop, A sheep rolls and tumbles, Alone with the birds.
Fire, Flaming devils leap, Quickly devouring their prey, Then flicker away.
Water, lizards, that when you try to touch them, swoop away." (Vouix).

*****

"Rain:
Rain drops, dropping, on my head, just like needles and threads of the Ocean Blue
Water, dropping on my head, tear drops, falling on my cheeks
Can you see, those beautiful streaks
Can you get, that wonderful beat?
Rain drops, dropping, on my head." (Roger).

*****

"There is a place beyond the sun
That has been there since the world began
When a person dies, or is born
A little piece of this place is torn
A song comes out of the tear
Begging all on earth not to despair." (Suzi Mantele).

****

20. Assignment: "Man, What is He?"

Throughout history, people have asked this question. What do you think?

———————

"Man, what is he? A creature who has created his world and is now unknowingly destroying it. What is man? A being of whom we know not enough. Not enough to cure what he himself has invented. Man, this something of which has evolved throughout the centuries. Man, who is henceforth going to die. Man, who created such a thing as pollution that is killing our animals, our fish, our plants, and us! This is man. Man who himself knows what is to happen. This is man, who God has placed on our earth to rule it and now it is to be destroyed. Man, what fate is to be his?" (Emmy).

*****

"We Must Strive On.
Face facts and reality and don't turn your back and be a nobody.
Take chances, do your thing some times but not all the time.
Be yourself don't try to hide
in someone elses shadow.
Like an innocent baby
that nobody knows don't
be a momma's child always hanging on your mother's dress Set out with the world and be blessed by the Guest of the sky's crest and rest among the best.
Look into the future
and watch history repeat itself like no one else
Face facts and reality
don't be a nobody
Do what you want
See what life is all about
Take chances
be lifely
It doesn't mean you have to go on with life and. death

And you have to be very mighty to strive on to keep your feet on the ground and strive on as a man." (Roger)

*****

"The sand as smooth as a marble floor
With foot marks going to the door
A white winged bird
Flying high above.
The roar of the ocean
Shakes the sand
And the gulls fly higher
And disappears over the horizon.
As the gulls sleep
And the ocean roars
A tint of silver moonlight
Shows a man with a gun.
And the deer sleeps
While the man shoots
The deer awakens
At the sound of a shot close by
And only to find
Her baby has died.
The sun has set
And the deer have died
Man has eaten
And gone to bed.
Man awakens and says
What to do today
Shall I go hunting
Shall I go fishing, .
Now the sun will set again
And another deer has died
I go, to sleep without a care
Thinking only of myself." (Janie).

*****

"ALTAMONT SHIT:
I was listening to a live recording of the Stones at Altamont. Shit, I put myself in the mood of the people there and recognized that many people were beaten up and one kid was killed to that music.

The music reflects this. It, like the day, is hot, sticky and violent. A very heavy, upper, downer, drunkas- hell, Red Mountain [cheap wine]AMPHETOMENMETHODRINEPHENOBARBILALBARBITURATE, trip.

It might be the race track. Think of the horrible vibrations that a race track generates. The whole mood changed when the area was changed from Sear's Point to Altamont. That, and the music and the people (leeches) and the Hell's Angels (ornerous motherfuckers or shitkickers stupendous) led to a killing, a death, a lot of broken heads and a shitty afternoon.

There was complete exploitation of it. All of the conservative newspapers decided to be accepted as hip so they played it up like: "Aside from a murder, a death and some maiming, it was a good rock show."

The pop A.M. radio stations said, "Allnightallofyougroovyflowerpeopleletsgotoarockshow but remember KFRCgivesyoufirstcoverageinallrockconcerts."

When will people learn you can't sell love, and hired hog riders can be worse than pigs." (Adam).

*****

"Roses are white and sometimes black,
Violets are purple, they don't have the knack.
Carnations are yellow and sometimes red,
I guess the whole world is like a flower bed.
Roses to the left, violets to the right,
And all us carnations get pushed out of sight.
And as you will know, if you don't know now,
The bad weeds they never get rid of somehow.
Now the grass--that's a different tune,
I bet you it will all be smoked very soon." (Suzi Mantele).

*****

"People:

Its not your fault some people just don't have class. Some make it if they try. Some's gonna stick to the bottom. Some people will rise from that gutter, only to fall onto their faces in a puddle of piss on the sidewalk. You just ain't got class. Some does and some don't. And you can't buy class. And whatever you don't have, don't come with money or sharp clothes.

Well that brave, hero, soldier boys' gon'na die and someones gonn'a stay a lot happier where they is. And you just ain't got no class (whatever that is).

Some's got soul and some's hip and others is drunk while Fred is stoned. And some people are dead afore they're born, and some's as good as dead, and some's gonn'a be real good, bigtime, classyassed, hot shit, gamblin man. This cat here's born to lose.

Some's a gutter boy, always was, always will be. He likes it that way. He don't mind old butts. He likes his wine sweet. He don't give an ole' damn about that piece o'meat.

Some's an all around boy. Some's a true Amerakan. This boy he likes to kick shit, like some what's stuck to the bottom. You can watch out for that boy.

Some's a bad motorcycleman, some's a good guy on a motorcycle. Some's cop, some's dead, some's soldier, some's right, some's wrong." (Adam).

*****

"The other night I watched a movie about a man who was going to be executed for murder. They showed him in the gas chamber sitting in the chair going to be gassed and there were windows all around him. Can you believe it, windows with people looking in at him. People just staring at him.

This country is going to kill you, but they can't give you any privacy. Ya know, "freedom of the press." What kind o' bull is that?" (Emily Marie).

*****

"I think that people should, I wish they would, stop being such assholes and not have more children than they can support. Life in the ghettos where people's wives, who don't take the pill, end up with all these stupid starving kids. Then they say that its other people fault for them being so poor. They like to have fun fucking but instead of using any kind of contraceptive they have the stupid kids instead. They lose money and are forced into worse living conditions with each kid they have. And who pays for their blunders but the taxpayer. The world has enough people and problems ahead, especially the ghetto people. They hardly ever get very significant income and they still have babies which gives them headaches, unbalances their budget, and god knows what else.

I'm not quite sure why these fools keep on having these damn kids. If they could support these kids that wouldn't be so bad but then, again, there would be the all-over problem of over population and the skyrocketing of supermarket prices.

If everybody had, say, more than two kids, they would be forcing the prices of everything up. Houses would be built all over the place on what's left of the countryside and I'd rather be dead than surrounded by all those people. Its already bad enough." (Joe Fork).

*****

"Me, myself, I don't think men can live in without killing people because men are being killed in other parts of the United States. Men are being killed in wars in other places. There will never be peace between men because somehow a war is going to break out between one country and another. Today we are trying to out-smart another so we can take over another country or something. Every man is fighting to get on top to be a leader. Once this man succeeds he might get killed in his home because another man wants to get on top the same way he did. There will never be peace between men." (Jake Smoot).

*****

"Why are people the way they are? People no longer seem to have any sense or feeling anymore. They know that they're screwing up our whole environment but they keep on doing the same things that made it that way. Things always look good at a distance but when you get closer, it looks worse. That's how things were a while ago. But now! Everything looks horrible.

Lets' get back to happy things. We've still got wind and boats and mountains. They're just a little dirty, that's all.

There are some things that really bother me. One is an item I saw in Time. An actress (rich) named Gina Lolosome- body had a coat made of ten wild tiger skins. There are only six hundred of these tigers known to be living on this planet. Therefore, their species is just a bit closer to extinction because of this stupid woman that doesn't even need that coat.

There's so much "occupant" and "resident" mail going around that junk mail is no longer a joke. My family gets Monkey Ward ads, Penny's ads and many ads for things that must have just been invented.

I've been reading all these little columns like "Dear Abby" and they are really stupid. People write in looking for help for some type of problem concerning other people (this seems stupid in the first place) and then some bitchy little old lady gives them some smarty-ass answer. They probably feel worse after the "help." I have a real old paper and "Dear Abby" looks older than she does now, about fourteen years later. I can't write the things I'd like to in this paper." (Lief Erickson).

*****

"There are more bad people than good.
There are more selfish people than good.
There are more people who don't realize things than people who do.
There are more violent people than there are non-violent.
For example: Kent State, MLK, Washington D.C., everywhere."
(Rabbit Paranoia).

*****

"Prostitutes:

I think pimps are stupid and so are prostitutes. To me pimps are stupid because if they wanted some money they could get out and work for it their self.

Prostitutes are stupid because if they had any sense she would stop working for men using their body for nothing and if she comes up pregnant her pimp would kick her ass.

My opinion is, I wouldn't ever want to be a prostitute because I know what they have to go through. They don't care who they go to bed with as long as they're making some money. Some go hungry from not eating and if they get a lot of money, like a hundred dollars (I doubt if they ever get up to that much) some pimps give their women just enough to pay their rent or to eat out and the pimps don't care how they look. I know a lot of girls who used their bodies and got pregnant and then went out and get abortions. And abortions are bad.

Some prostitutes try and steal their food and their clothing but if they get caught doing it that would give them a record. If they try to get a job that would be an affect on her." (Little Green Man).

*****

"The world is sick, the people are sick. But why? I like life but sometimes I just get sick of it. If only people could learn to live together without fighting and hating each other. I want to get married but I hope when I get married the world will be a better place to live in." (Shirley).

*****

"It makes me sick to see all these people going around with hate in their minds. They hate people who look (color) different, dress different, talk, see, think or smell different I guess its the difference that counts (to them).

They are usually showing off, its true, but, it is such a stupid way to show-off. They're wasting their minds acting cool in following crowds. They are noisy, boisterous and very inconsiderate of their fellow man, even their brothers and sisters. They find delight is stirring up a fight and ugly repulsive things. Of course, if people like killing and hate I guess I can't change their opinions and ideas, but I sure wish I could." (Eleanor Hume).

*****

"I'm going to write about religion and the churches. There are some people in the churches who say that you don't come to church every Sunday you will not be saved. This is not true because when the Lord God made Adam and Eve he saw to it that they learn no evil. Now people must learn that going to church will not save you. If you think about it, no church is different.

Now when talking about being saved some people are nothing but hypocrites. I have seen a lot of them. The only perfect person that God put on this earth was Jesus. His mother, Mary, was a virgin and his father, Joseph, was a prophet. These people are wonderful to read about. Also God." (Somon Marie).

*****

"A Thought
I look up in the sky
and I begin to wonder why
Why people do the things they do
because it affects me and you." (Tony Jackson).

****

21. *"Black and White."*
As Martin Luther King was one of the first desegregated school, inter-racial relations were on everyone's mind.

"Colors are Beautiful but they Hate one another. I had problems on the day the kids from Kentfield school visited. In a discussion we had, I brought out a point: The black kids call white kids names--whites grin and bear it, but if a white kid calls a black kid anything, not even a racist name — out they go with bloody noses, broken legs, arms, anything.

Then a few of the seventh grade black boys (who shouldn't have been there), started saying I had called them racist names and afterward they came back and gave me a bit of trouble. Well, that's life, but I wish someone could wipe racism off the face off of the earth. (Not for public use.)." (Anon).

*****

"We give them the answers but they don't understand
The Artist paints a picture
or he makes a photograph
and no one understand him
its just another fad
And loving is for fools
And money come from war
And the poet speaks of loving
And they thro him out the door
Ooh again

So the dancer dances lightly creating thoughts so clear
But they close their eyes
And spit on him
And no ones there to care

Who moves among the shadows

like a sniper in the dust
Its just another child who's very cold and lost." (Adam).

*****

"I love you
Say you love me too
say its true say you do
The sky is black
the clouds are blue
Black is beautiful
and so are you
A black mountain in the sky
the summer breeze coming by
and in the sky a black butterfly
A black horse in the street he as fine as can be
I wish it was me.
A black man in jail
he is Huey and
someone else.
A Black man in the south he knows what its all about Black is beautiful but not the South." (Jack).

*****

"Soul: Many people think that blacks are the only people who have soul. Well that is true to a certain extent. Anyone can have soul. In my book all you have to do is think black, be able to rap about black people's life, and most of all, to live like a black. You also have to deal with black music, as they call it, soul music. What do I mean by this? Well, you have to like it.

In some Black churches that you go in you might hear a preacher saying, "Deep down in your soul you know that you are a Christian." Well, that's the same thing that we Blacks say about soul food. But, only we say that it is satisfying to your soul.

I think that there is no woman in the world who can cook like a Black sister can. That sister don't have no recipe she just slap something together. When its through cooking they got what we call soul food. If you do find a woman that can cook like a sister can, let me know.

Now, since I have talked about soul and soul food I guess I'll talk about soul music. These are some names of records that we call soul music: *Psychedelic Shack, Cloud Nine, A Chair is Still a Chair, Yesterday, Hey Jude, Didn't I, A.B.C., Who,s Loving You, I Want You Back, The' Touch of You, I'm Just a Prisoner, The Best Part of a Love Affair is Breaking*, and lots more.

Now all these records that I have listed are records that really get down in your soul. It really makes you think about your love or your used-to-be love. Not only do they make you. think about that, they make you think of other things, like dancing, singing, acting, playing and many other things.

All these things that I have talked about all add up to SOUL baby and there is no doubt about this. In the near future you are going to witness a social change and a half. Whether or not you will be able to adapt to this change will depend on how well educated you are to the economic and social conditions. of this day. SOUL BABY, NO JIVE." (Doris).

*****

"Black and darkness equal death
Black is like a motherless child
In the Ghetto
Black is like the night with no end
Black is a person
with no destination
Black is like a man
with just darkness
never to step
out into the guiding light
Black is where
there is no where
no silvery meadow
no blossoms and rose and violets

Black is just the night easing
up on death
like a spirit in the dark chamber
of life and death
you just know the rest." (Roger).
*****

"Black is beautiful
That I know
Black is beautiful
So my skin shows
I went to the rock

To hide my face
The rock cried out
No hiding place
Ghetto what it is
Place of shame
Place of horror
Place of fear
That what it is?

White folks fly
Here am I
White folks flee
Still there is me." (Penny).
*****

"True or False?
Black is the night
Light is the day
Dirty is the ghetto
Where the black children play
Clean are the streets
Where the white people walk
They don't have a worry

All they do is talk
While the black man works hard
On the job all day
The white sits at a desk
For his pay." (Tony Jackson).

*****

"Sambo":
Hey Nigger! Hey Whitey!
Hey there young man
Sambo's coming
Run as fast as you can
You better get out the street
You better run fast
Sambo's coming
He's going to kick your ass
Sambo is the baldest
Sambo is the best
He's going to deal with you
Like he dealt with the rest." (Tony Jackson).

*****

"Do You Realize
Black is the color
Everyone knows
Black is beautiful
And so is soul
Black people have rhythm
They can also dance
They could make it but
They don't get a chance
Take those rich white people
They can't do a thing
But its the black people
Who can dance and sing." (Tony Jackson).

*****

"MAN...has been around for a short while. White man has been around for an even shorter while. White man has destroyed or damaged almost everything beautiful and then taught nonwhite, non-destructive people how to destroy what's beautiful. White race I denounce you. I no longer want to be white.

I've been thinking about this revolution thats happening now. If some fat hairy motherfucker was beating on my friend, sister, brother, girlfriend I would kill them. If they pulled out a pistol or a rifle I would use a machine gun." (Adam).

*****

"Profile of a black man, so proud and beautiful. He is starting to rebel against the way he is being treated. I know so many people that have died. I don't want to go to any more funerals." (Emily Marie)

*****

"Black magic is tragic
like tragedy
that never ends
it's like getting on a merry-go-round
that starts at the end
Where there isn't a friend
and no Sun." (Roger).

*****

"Happiness: If love ruled the world there wouldn't be any more fighting and killing and black and white would learn to get along with each other. To me, black and white are the only two races that can't get along together. I wish these people would try and get together." (Little Green Man).

*****

"Life is day and night ,white and black and red yellow, brown. Life is being in the dark or the light, right or wrong, strong or weak, retreat or defeat. Life or death heaven or hell God or Satan." (Roger).

*****

"Listen people
He ain't no slave no more
He's moving up in the world
And that's for shore." (Tony Jackson).
*****

"Black Rage
Black Rage is caused
By the white pig
When he beats up our old
And chases our kids
For the pigs are the ones
Who bring black rage on strong
They put us in jail
So the black rage will be gain
Black Rage is something
That cannot be controlled
Its been in the ghetto
Heaven knows how long." (Tony Jackson).
*****

"One Black Night:
Now that the day has gone
The black night rolls along
A lot of black figures
Run through the ghetto
For what is happening is mellow
For the night in Watts
Just after the day
Is frightening everyone away
Burn Baby Burn is the cry
They are burning Watts
Now, don't you know why?" (Roger).
*****

"That steel hurts my brother's back
That glass cuts my hand

Cement blisters my feet
Wood suits me fine
The water its a'boilin
And life gets no longer
Meat for the rich
An cake for the poor
With wire for your neck
And chains for your ankles
Fly in your jet plane
While the ghetto burns lower
Livin free is illegal
The freer you live
The deader you'll be." (Adam).

*****

"Black Man's World:
The world today
Is as plain as can be
It's a black man's world
Can't you see
Black is beautiful
like the night so still
and real Black is like
a Gospel song so
long but not wrong
so don't sing no pitiful song
 Black is alone its not wrong to sing a black song." (Roger).

*****

"I think that jobs should be offered to everyone. There should be no color involved. But some people don't think so; they always look at a black person--the way he or she dresses and the way we talk.

   Now, up against some white people we look right-on and some white people make us look bad. We are gonna move on up. It takes time. You ought to check out Putney Swope. The white people felt sorry for him and they gave him the majority of the votes. He also moved on up.

It will take a lot of time for everyone to recognize us. People must really know that we ain't made to work on plantations. We were all created equal and we (as black people) would like a chance to prove it. We want everything that's good coming to us. We only want a chance to prove to you that we can do what's right. Give us a chance." (Somon Marie).

*****

"Everybody is a star
It doesn't matter what you want to be
To me it matters what you are
Everybody is a star
when you grow up, if you ever,
you will be a star
man or woman
black or white
you are a star." (Roger).

*****

"I have a dream,
Black and White children, Walking, Hand in Hand.
Looking for what Moses Called the Holy Promised Land
Where Jesus came down, and was made man,
By the Father's open right hand." (Roger).

*****

"*Ebony, Look, Life*, which would you rather have,
Before our friends take over." (Puddingtang).

*****

"White:
White is a color. White is a shame. White is hateful, White is lovely. Just like me."
Baby:
Black Baby, Black Baby, Where do you live?
up hill down hill, all around

If you don't believe me
I will scream a little louder
Black:
Black is the
color just like
white. Dig it. " (Francis).

*****

"Black and White
Black and White
Are different in ways, color is one
But a man's character pays
Most black men are funny
Most white men are stern
But both of their children
Come to school to learn
What they learn at school
Ain't no damn golden rule
Its black and white relations
Now that's cool." (Tony Jackson).

*****

"..or how about the Indians? The Indians own this whole damned country in the first place. Well, I doubt they would even want to rule this country.
But they should...and they should send us all back to where we came from...Hell! (Emily Marie).

****

22. Assignment: The "Generation Gap)

Recently there has been a lot of talk in the newspapers and on T.V. about the "generation gap". What do you understand these words to mean? What are your ideas on this topic?

"When you finally see how really stupid you are.
When you think you're inferior and you know you are.
When you got those fire hydrant blues.
When you hardly realize you're there and you want to call a friend who will tell you how great you are but you don't cause they won't. And you have five pages of hard solid math to do and you didn't do many of the things around the house that you're supposed to. There's nothing like parents not to understand." (Adam).

*****

"There are a lot of changes to look forward to. There aren't too many people who believe that this change is coming. But me and my other friends sometimes talk about it and we believe that change is coming.

    I for myself think that some of the people in the world won't believe anyone. They are too busy drinking, cursing and doing other sinful things. I don't follow what some people do because you can get in serious trouble. They always want to set an example for younger people. But instead of setting the right example they set the wrong.

    When it is too late to try and change the younger kids, they wonder what's wrong and what happened to make them do wrong. They really don't realize that the kids have seen too much. The parents do things in front of their kids that they are sorry for later.

    Let us hope when this change does come that people will change also. Let us hope. If we don't look out something will turn out bigger than expect. People one day are going to wake up to another day and another time. Not knowing what is going to happen to them when they step out of their door. It could even happen when you are in your house. What they don't realize about this change is that people don'ts, or won't, wake up to the fact that change is going to come. When it does come it will be too late for those people to realize what is going on." (Somon Marie).

******

"You know, you're right. About parents I mean. It is their hang-up. I've been watching them and listening. Oh shit have I been listening. They give you all the shit which they would force on you even if you didn't want it and then they yell at you cause you don't act grateful.

I wouldn't trade them in for anything because they did put me together and I am a little fond of them. I think the only reason they yell at me is because they raised me and they realize (or just think) that its all their fault.

Well, how irresponsible I am all of a sudden; ever since I wanted to break away a little. It is because I really am irresponsible or because they don't want me to break away or both?" (Adam).

*****

"Well, I am going to give my opinion on how the generation gap starts with the teenagers. It starts when the teenagers are small and they can't buy the things they want, when the parents wouldn't let them buy it with their own money.

When they get older they get madder and madder about the same thing over and over again so they have arguments with each other that keeps on happening everyday so they go out on a date with a girl or boy and don't come back when they should.

And another thing is when the parents smoke cigarettes and when their teenagers start smoking they say it's bad for the lungs and the kidneys. But, when the teenagers say that to their parents they will probably say because we are adults we can smoke. So sometimes the teenagers probably smoke anyway.

So the teenagers go on to higher things like drugs but when they're hooked it's too late to stop so probably by then the parents should know about him or her taking drugs. Then the parents takes him or her to the hospital to see if they can make them stop taking it. When they stop taking drugs they probably go back on it and so go to juvenile hall for a year. And it happens over again until the doctors give him something to stop it for good." (Fu Manchu).

*****

"The young people of today are the only ones who can change the system the older people screwed up. The older people have made this system one of racism, capitalism and suppression. Like the black people are suppressed and racism is being used on them. They work hard at their jobs to help get a better economy for the white man and get paid very little, while the white man has all the money they want (that is most white people) but there are some white people who are starving so it is a two way street.

This is what the older people of this country have done. They just plain messed it up. That's why its up to all the young people in this country to change it into a democracy like it was supposed to be in the first place.

I don't know how they are going to do it but what ever means necessary should be the way they do it, because that's the only way they can beat the system of the United States of America. They will probably have to resort to violence and that is really the only way they can do it. That is just my own personal feelings about the way they might have to do it.

When I say "young people" I mean people as young as me. We have just got to get our thing together between ourselves or else we will be living in the same kind of world that we are living in now and I personally don't want that kind of World. Well, that's just the way I feel about the world and the young people who have to change it." (Ian).

*****

"Equality: When will we be together, the young and the old? Do we always have to disagree with them? Do they always have to disagree with us? Let me tell you, all we need is more togetherness like the Russians they spend more time with their young ones." (Jake Brown).

*****

"Well, I think little kids are all right, they even sometimes have good ideas. But grown-ups just don't give them a chance. Grown-ups aren't always right. But, you can't tell them that. They say they know what's best. That's not true. If they would only give us a chance." (Pamela Marie).

*****

"The reason why I don't know so much about the Generation Gap is because I didn't know a thing about it. I thought it was a television show.

I don't see why they call themselves the "generation gap," because it is not really a gap to me. It is just a large bunch of kids (young men and young women) who want their voices heard." (Kimberly).

****

23. "Getting Stoned."
While a certain group at the school smoked marijuana daily, there was no evidence of "hard" drugs. However, this topic, more than any other, was the subject of what can be called "a conspiracy of ignorance." From the students point of view.....

───────────

"When you got a lid you got new friends." (Adam).
*****
"I don't see why everybody is making such a big fuss over drugs. I know that they have been going around for a long time and people are finally doing something about it.

Why did the U.S. hassle Switzerland and all the other foreign countries about the heroin and speed, acid etc., that was floating by the authorities. Do they think that just because its not going to be so easy to get by importation that it will stop all or most of the drug using in the U.S. and Canada?

If anything, it will just tempt young people to try to bring it through. Most of them might get through but the ones that get caught will tempt others to try it. Then the U.S. will really be in trouble up to their neck. There will be more drug using and more young people caught. Just think, if all the young people were in jail, who would fight the wars?" (Suzi Mantele).
*****
"I think marijuana should definitely be made legal. Its really sort of ridiculous to stop a human being from doing what he or she wants to. Especially when there's no danger in the act of smoking marijuana.

Marijuana to me seems to help a lot of people, in fact, its proven an excellent relaxant and tranquilizer. It seems like when people smoke it they don't go out and kill people or get in accidents. They usually just go somewhere and enjoy themselves.

Probably if younger people were in government today marijuana would be legal by now. But, since we have all older people working with government we will probably have to wait an extra five years or so.

At least the older people are finally starting to realize that the law preventing marijuana is ridiculous, so it will probably be made legal pretty soon." (Sarah Richardson).

*****

"How to Make the Most of Your Lid: The first thing you do even before you buy is smoke some. If he won't let you--don't buy. "When in doubt don't deal." Make sure there's enough grass there. The primary way to make the most of your lid is to buy a big lid.

Now take your lid and spread it onto a piece of white paper so as not to lose any. Take as many seeds and stems out as possible. Shake stems over grass. Put stems and seeds aside in separate boxes.

Over another piece of white paper pour grass from last paper into fine-mesh strainer. Do not throw-away last paper. Push grass through strainer onto paper. Take all seeds and stems left and put them in their seed and stem boxes. Without loosing any shake grass around on the paper for a little while. Pour grass into jar or bottle that doesn't narrow at the top and will be small enough to pour easily, and with control of how much, into cigarette papers. Don't throw away that paper or turn it upside down either. Don't even blow on them.

With a dull knife scrape lightly over paper. A yellow dust will remain. It's pollen. Put pollen into very small jar. The pollen is far out. Put the tiniest pinch into your hash pipe (I use tweezers) and take. You'll only get one hit no matter how much you put in. It'll get you stoned like hashish and lasts about two hours varying with how much you smoke.

Chop your stems up and save they can be smoked in a long stemmed pipe or in a hookah. Don't use papers for stems 'cause you'll burn the hell out of your throat.

Smoking Your Grass: Your grass is best enjoyed in papers I do not advise a pipe because of those valuable resins. Instead of a roach clip save a small bottle and before the roaches burn your lips, put them in. When all your grass is gone take all the grass out of the papers and re-roll. I haven't figured out what to do with papers just don't leave any grass sticking to them. You can save these roaches too and the more times the roaches are saved the stronger the grass. Roach weed is one hit weed.

Now take your seeds (the darker ones are best) and soak them overnight in water. Then put them between two pieces of wet cloth or paper towel. In a week all that will sprout have sprouted. Plant them in a shallow box with slightly sandy soil. Try to put them in the soil that you will transplant them into. Water every day or so.

If you want a truly powerful crop put them in a glass enclosed fish tank, or the like, with glass or saran wrap on top. When the plants are fairly tall and have a lot of leafy green on them they are ready to transplant. Plant them carefully and when they are young (even before transplantation) water at the base for the water rots the stem and they die.

Getting good grass; the three R's are: They like lots of Sun, Water and Love. All plants are sensitive to human feelings. Hate has even been known to kill plants. When they are tall (grass grows as much as six feet and larger) and are a dark green. You can pick them. Before picking get pollen! Hang the plants upside down so all the resins can run to the leaves and flowers. Flowers are the best part. Some people keep only the flowers.

Warning! Don't pick the male plant because you can't get high from it. The male is much straighter and stronger than the female and doesn't have very big flowers. It is also much less attractive than the female. Also keep plants protected from little beasties which just love cannabis. Put wire around them or else don't stop watching them. Even cats have been known to eat dope. The Danger of Marijuana! Getting busted." (Adam).

*****

"Today I met an old friend of mine who I haven't seen in two years. Her name is Ginger. When she was in sixth grade, she went to this school. We became very good friends.

In all the time we knew each other, we never visited each other's houses. One time she did come out to Muir Beach. It was boiling hot and we went swimming in all our clothes because neither of us had bathing suits and we didn't want to conform to no clothes like almost everyone else.

Once Ginger came to school wearing black leather boots similar to the ones I own at present. She had received them from her parents for Christmas I remember how she gushed and gushed about them. She was really happy about them.

My most vivid memories are of the times Ginger and I would discreetly hide Marlboro cigarettes in our socks, smuggle them into school and smoke them warily after school. There was this one tree where we went to smoke. Then I would really have to run to catch my bus.

Man, we thought we were so cool. Smoking cigarettes. Super cool. As I think back, boy, what a bummer. We had our heads on all wrong.

Then Ginger moved to L.A.. Down there she skipped from seventh to eighth grade. She visited some friends at Tam. Valley and I saw her at Muir Beach. She was living in a nice spot and owned a horse. Things sure sounded rosy until she rosily told me she'd taken her first acid trip. Two, in fact. I was really stunned. Now, there was a gap between us. I had had my kicks with cigarettes and pot, but I quit. I didn't think that Ginger would, but all along I knew I would never go past pot." (New York, New York).

*****

"Did you know that it's a real beautiful world? Well it is, if you go up on top of a mountain side and look down on a beautiful sunny day after it has rained and you smell the brisk air and see the blooming flowers you will see exactly what I mean. In a way it kind of gets you stoned off nature.

Another far-out thing to do would be to take a walk in the rain and pick sour grass and flowers and watch how the water hits them. It's really out-of-sight!

But my favorite thing to do is to sit up in a field of sour grass (I really dig sour grass) and look at the bay. You really don't need grass to get you stoned--you can get stoned more easily of nature and the beautiful world, don't you try it?" (Suzi Mantele).

*****

"Yah, its Gonn'a Get You Too
It fills your mind
and
Sets your veins aglow
It creeps and crawls
and
Jumps inside and dark whole
It's warm an' hot
Oh
It burns your soul
(in a nice sort of way)
If you're paranoid
it's
Gonn'a dribble under your
door
Pretty soon its gonn'a
leap out
and
scream
Hallelujah!" (Adam).

*****

"The Fate of a Fool: I am an ass. Yesterday I met a college kid who's living next door who wanted to get stoned. So, having some dope (grass), I took him up on the mountain and a couple of kids in a car said, "Wann'a smoke some dope?" So we got in and went up the dirt road. We smoked about four joints. The two guys in the car didn't take much because they were on acid. Then my friend took out a small bottle that contained D.C.T., which you smoke. He said that he guaranteed us that we wouldn't want more than one toke.

I, not knowing what it was besides being a new chemical, naturally smoked some. Now then again, if I had known what it was I might not have lit any. But, since I didn't know the first thing about it, naturally, I had to.

I went home and had to talk to my parents first. Oh shit. I almost blew it when my dad asked me a question and I forgot it but at the last instant I remembered. Whew! I looked at my eyes in the bathroom mirror and I've never seen any more red and dilated and completely fucked.

I went to bed and plunged through unknown universe of a new dimension. To anyone the dimension can only be described as more than three dimensional because every side had three dimensions to it too.

I described some of it on the paper I gave you Monday. I also had some very strange Zap comic-like hallucinations in the separate dimensions. See, I'm a crazy ass. Tell me something." (Adam).

****

24. Assignment: "Pollution"

In front of the school was a large lawn where students would often eat lunch, this often created problems as the garbage they left strewn around attracted seagulls.

One morning I collected half a dozen garbage cans and dumped their contents, (cafeteria refuse and all) in the middle of the classroom floor. The day was warm, the smell ripe.

On the blackboard was the message: "This is your garbage, what are you going to do about it, and all the other junk you create?"

"What you can do with the garbage is bury it where there is a place where no one will go. I couldn't stand the smell of it if it overcame the world. We would all be dead by millions of people getting sick from the smell of it, the looks of it and the pounds of it. Garbage really may overcome the world. If we burn it people will still die and the whole world will become polluted. Garbage will bury people. You got to get it before it gets you or you will be dead by garbage.   GARBAGE IS OVERCOMING THE WORLD." (Prudence).

*****

"Dear President Nixon,

I would like you to take out some of your time and read this letter because as you know we will be tomorrow's leaders. I think you should take time to read this letter if I took my time to write it.

The first fact, and the only fact that I would like to discuss, is about the pollution, because I am young and I'm not ready to die yet! Also, I know that there is a whole lot of more people that isn't ready to die yet.

I know, and I know that you know, that there has to be some way to stop pollution. You have all of the money, so why don't you do something about pollution. It might be hard to do but I believe that something can be done.

Well, this is all I have to say for now but when I get a little older I will be calling on you again.

(I didn't mail this letter because I found out that pollution can't be stopped. The only reason we have pollution is because of people and the population keeps growing strong. So the only thing I can think of is try to stop the rapid increase in the population growth and fast too.)" (Tamila Shalon).

*****

"Several of the students at MLK are two-faced. They scream about ecology and the need for more grass, and then they go and rip up grass and throw it at each other and have fun doing it.

They scream, "Look what you dirty pigs are doing to America, you're polluting it," and then they go outside for lunch and throw their brown paper lunch bags on the ground and walk away. They can run, jump and wrestle but they are always too tired to walk to the garbage can.

They say stop the DDT and pesticides, they are killing our birds and then they go out and feed the seagulls and then kill them with rocks.

Then comes apathy. You tell them, "You stupid fools, you are destroying your environment just like the rest of America! So, you have no right to scream." They say, "Yeh, yeh, listen to President Nixon. Next we have Spiro Agnew." Then they go back to ripping up the grass and throwing it at each other.

They scream, "Stop destroying this country you capitalists, you'll kill us all." Then they go out to lunch and kill seagulls, rip up plants, roots and all, and leave their garbage on the ground and not in the trash can.

I myself am probably guilty of many of these crimes. As is the case with most people I don't mean to do it, but it gets done. The incidents described above have all happened in the last two days." (Simon).

*****

"How beautiful it would be to fly. To float in the air and be blown by the wind. It is beautiful for man to a- achieve and if we had been put on earth to fly we would have wings. But we have to make a machine that flies. Its bad enough to make something to fly in, but we also have to ruin the air so you can't breathe. We are so worried about us not being able to breathe from air pollution or not having any water to drink because it all has oil in it. Well, what about animals? What about them suffocating, or dying be-cause the oil has ruined their wings so they can't fly then they are drowned. Why should they suffer when it is you and me who are polluting everything. We are our own enemies." (Emily Marie).

*****

"The Bay
Once Beautiful as the Ocean
Whales once inhabited it
Crabs were once abundant The Bay was as beautiful As the blue ocean, now look at it.

Then the Golden Gate Bridge came, many men died building it, the big iron bridge is a beauty but, it was not there once. The whales looked more beautiful than the bridge but it helps to transfer people from one side to the other." (Jake Brown).

*****

"It scares people to think about the possibility of the human race going extinct. They say there is nothing they can do about it. But, what people, if any at all, understand it is they who are causing it. All forms of garbage (smog, sewage, etc.,) is slowly but surely killing us, and it is picking up speed as it goes along. Before long we will have no drinking water, no air to breathe and no place to live; it will all be covered with garbage dumps and sewage buildings.

People have been working on the problem of garbage and have come up with: making buildings out of it; making it into cubes; covering it with a chemical that helps fish and dump it in the water;

disintegrate it; and others. All terribly expensive and none without faults.

Garbage maybe taken into space soon, which is still not the answer to smog, but anything would be a help. Considering the earth's state now, we may never make it." (Sir Genius).

*****

"Crappy Poems.
I. Mary had a little lamb,
It's feces white as snow.
And every time that Mary stopped,
That lamb was sure to go.
II. There's something happening
It will catch your eye.
A shower of H-bombs in the sky,
Man's paradise is going.
Ka-flush!
III. Beat heads, one, two,
Lets take a trip to the Raguly Zoo.
Chitter, chatter, rackety-yack.
When you talk to the animals,
They talk back.
IV. No one could beat,
That funny old man on the toilet seat.
Citizens would spit in his eye,
But he was too sly.
He opened his hole,
Reached in his bowl,
And gave them back their own crap." (Fritz the Cat).

*****

"Pipes
Pipes for heat
Pipes for cold
Pipes for water
Pipes for air

Pipes for blood
Pipes for transportation
Pipes or communication
Pipes for bullets
Pipes for fluids.
It seems everything is made up of pipes. Weird?" (Rabbit Paranoia).

*****

"The plant stands alone, surrounded by dirt unprotected from all enemies no matter who, how, or when.
A human walks by, unaware he picks a green leaf
and destroys life in his hands, now part of the living thing is dead.
The smog floats by
It too destroys life
the plant is suffocating
now most of the plant is dead.
A small fire starts near by
the burning plant has no place to escape to. It cannot run now nothing but ashes remain.
The living plant is no more." (Dusty).

******

"Lazy, hazy, tired, ol', sad, slow, nice and sleepy day.
Today ain't been much. I woke up and started walkin down that road where I met some kids I knew, smoking some dope for Earth Day. Hallalooja. Other than that the day was pretty unsensational. I was tired when we went down to the Bay. Its an old bay now. Ahh, if I could see the sunrise on that bay a couple of years ago-- before the days of pollution and destruction. When there were beaches on the now- filled edges of that cesspool called Richardson Bay. Before the white man, when the water was clear and myriad birds flocked to its blue-green waters. Someday (or maybe somewhere) that bay will once again run clear.

The wind flows in from the sea over the mountains. It is power, force, strength. It carries the fog across the Bay. Beautiful, peaceful, violent. It was here before you. It will remain here long after you no one can stop it! Man can stop or control almost everything. They can chart it, forecast it, usually protect themselves from it, but they can't stop it.

So, fuck you Flood Control. Up yours Highway Department." (Adam).

*****

"Deep ocean
blue sky
be my guide
to a new true and beautiful sky
Deep ocean
Blue sky
Be blessed by the eyes of God
Deep ocean
Blue sky
Be my guide." (Roger).

*****

"This is a poem about our field trip, though very brief it is.
Dear nature
many people love you
more people couldn't care less
but to see you being used and cared
for is beautiful
but thrown about and for money
is very ugly." (Rabbit Paranoia).

*****

"San Francisco Bay. One of the things I know is that the Bay is beginning to stink and I think that sea animals are becoming scarce. Sea animals like crabs which were once very abundant in the Bay, and shrimp also, are scarce with all that pollution. The entire Bay is becoming filled in at the bottom with all kinds of waste. The beach is very nice looking by the Golden Gate, but all that beauty that was there a long time ago is not there anymore." (Jake Brown).

******

"Polluted Poetry: Before, freshness in the air and everywhere
Clear water for everyone to drink
People zooming in the air
Flying high and watching things shrink.
After
Filth, filth, in the sky
Everyone on earth will die
Living creations will flee from the smell
Because living in a world of pollution
Is like living in a world of hell.
1976
Roses are red, violets are blue,
The birds are dead,
And humanity is too.
All because of man's mistake,
Years ago.
He should'da used chicken shit
To make his cars go.
End
Roses are dead
Violets are dead
Murder at your feet,
Children playing around the corpses
Which lay in silence on every street.
*Chicken shit: Good element for making cars run. Man on news said he gets about thirty miles to the gallon and cost about one penny per gallon. It hardly pollutes the air at all." (Fitz the Cat).

*****

"What do I see? I see the people and my own shadow. What do I feel? The coolness of the grass and the wind and the warmth of the sun. What do I smell? People smell, grass smell. What do I hear? Car, people, the wind whistling in my ear. The colors of our world are brown and green But will it become concrete?." (Rabbit Paranoia).

*****

"The Sea
The sea is a very mellow thing
It makes a person want to sing
It flings it's waves upon the rocks
It scares the people on the docks.
It's filled with fish and minnows too
It filled with food for me and you
So love the sea with all your heart
I hope that it will never part." (Tony Jackson).

*****

"The mountains are hidden
Beneath that killer smog
As smoke billows forth
The sky sometimes blue
Is now covered with haze
It may be forever." (Dusty).

*****

"Big city hot with smog. Busses, taxies and cars. One lonely fly with nowhere to go but into an old kitchen in an old apartment to visit a rat." (Maria).

****

25. Assignment: "The State of the Union."

Periodically the President gives a "State of the Union" speech; what is your opinion?

"Does anyone in politics know really what is going on in this country? Have any of them grown up in a ghetto? Were their parents farm workers?

People talk a lot you know. Like everyone in the political business has to gain the people's vote. They didn't live in a slum, their parents had a good paying job. They had enough money to get their son through a good college and into politics. Few people in this country ever thought about anything else but money.

With all the thirty-six presidents (or however many there've been) have any of them been black? We brought the black man here against his will, the least we can do is let him be in politics.

The country you and me live in was stolen. Oh well, we killed most of the Indians off so we don't have to worry about that. Maybe when we get old enough to rule the country we can give peace a chance. If the world hasn't ended by then maybe we will give it a try." (Emily Marie).

*****

"I was thinking of writing a story about a boy in the future who was scared because in the streets below the national guard was shooting all long-hairs and all non-whites they could see.

That reminded me of the book *It Can't Happen Here* by Sinclair Lewis. I had been thinking that the story would never happen and the book showed that even in Amerika, especially in Amerika, dictatorship would be endured because the people think Amerika is perfect. Any crisis couldn't happen to them and they would put up with it because they thought that next week, or month, or year, things would have all calmed down.

Then I realized that it is happening right now only I don't know who the dictator is." (Washington Irving).

*****

"If America is all that beautiful why is it we have all these minute men and other crime organizations always trying to kill or threaten someone just because they believe or back-up what they have to say. But all I have to say for the situation is that the people that are hurt in their young lives now are the people who will be coining down on the United States about twenty years later." (Edward).

*****

"The President of our mighty land talked. And as I looked upon his face with wonder, I saw not the face of the representative and leader of the American people, but something more like that of a court jester, or maybe a puppet.

Oh President, how undemocratic you are. You decide (for the good of the people) to kill for peace, against the will of the people. For shame, oh wicked President." (Adam).

*****

"Dear President Nixon,
Are you just going to sit up in the White House and do nothing? Have you been hearing about all these riots at the Universities?
Mr. Nixon, all you are doing is sending all your troops into these Universities to scare people. Just like the University of California. The pigs are there and they just be walking around hitting people in the head and they didn't even do anything.

At Kent State your national guard killed four people and they wasn't even doing anything." (Johnny).

*****

"The United States government is the same to me as it is always going to be, and that is nothing. This is because you and any other of my social science teachers haven't talked to us about it enough so that we can put it down on paper.

What I have learned about Democracy is different from what I think it is. All we learned out of them textbooks was that a Democracy is all those British laws and what British laws affect the communists [i.e., colonists] and it turned out to be a Democracy.

Well being black a democracy is a whole lot different from what we learned out of the book and as soon as I get the time I'm going to sit down and write it." (Tamila Shalon).

*****

"Police are always beating up people and possibly killing them, and they get away with this sort of thing.

I know a story that's true. It happened in Marin City about two or three years ago. A riot was going on late one night about two. It was a friend of mine, his name is Butch. Some police had shot him. Every time he would say something he got shot. He was shot about ten times in his legs and places.

Then he got put in Marin General Hospital for nine months or a year. After he got out he was a cripple for the rest of his life. He had to use the bathroom out of his side.

Another friend of mine was about seventeen years old and the police were trying to catch him. The police are supposed to give a warning before shooting. Soon as they saw him they started shooting. They even tried to run him down with their car. They finally caught him. They put him in the car and began beating him. He was handcuffed and nothing he could do." (Jake Smoot).

*****

"I watched President Nixon's speech on the war in Cambodia and it was really unbelievable. He assumed that everyone agreed with him: "I want to thank you for your support...." I have yet to go along with anything he has done.

If you think back he was the "peace" candidate and yet he is making a bigger war than there was.

If I am ever asked or told to fight in an American versus anybody war, I'm going to leave. I would leave now but, there is just no way I can. I do not like this country and I feel that any effort to change it is useless.

If the President doesn't care why should I. As far as I'm concerned he's in it for the money and nothing else. I'm really not saying anything that hasn't been said before, but there's not a hell of a lot to say. People say impeach Nixon, but then what about Agnew? Muskie?, Humphrey? I can't take this country or anybody in it seriously. They're all crazy." (Lief Erickson).

*****

"The United States is a country of racism, fascism, suppression, and many other things like that.

The United States suppresses many other races because of the color of their skin. They are blacks, yellow, red, etc., who live in dirty filthy places and are starving because the United States thinks that it is better than they are so they treat them like dogs.

The United States is so greedy for money that they would do anything to get it. They would even kill to get it as you see they are doing in Vietnam. Killing thousands of innocent people because they have Shell Oil plants over there and they are afraid the minority over there might try to take them over.

The United States already has so much money they don't know what to do with it. They spend millions of dollars sending men to the moon while they could be using it to help the starving people in the U.S.

It really aggravates me to see all the starving people in the United States when the United States has so much money. The U.S. worries about their money in other countries when it should be worrying about their own country's people. Someday the U.S. is going to fall to defeat." (Ian).

*****

"About a year ago our family took a vacation and went on a trip south. In the South we visited many places and saw many things but one thing troubled me.

In Georgia there is a gigantic blob of rock called Stone Mountain. The thing was gigantic. To me the thing was a thousand feet high and a billion feet wide. Of course, there was a corny little gift shop and a train that went a- round the base of Stone Mountain but neither of these tourist attractions hurt the mountain at all--except for one thing.

As you faced the mountain head from the main entrance you could plainly see a gigantic carving of civil war generals heading heroically into battle. The carving dwarfed the artists who were on a scaffolding balancing themselves with sand blasters and air pumps. About a hundred feet below them was (or still is) a tremendous amount of chipped rock.

In my opinion the carving wasn't very good. It was sort of done the way art was done during the civil war—sometimes called America's artless art. You know, the kind of painting done with the horses and riders stiff as a board in the heat of a battle with absolutely no expression on their faces.

This art is done in the same way. One general holds some reins with an oversized glove while another holds an empty revolver.

To me this whole thing is sick. Once again man blasts his mark into one of nature's greater creations and once again some great con artist convinces the population into giving them job security for the next decade or so, so they can scar the face of the earth with a horrible plaything they call "art." (Potassium Nacnud).

*****

"Are you proud of the country you live in? Are you? I'm not. It was such a beautiful country. The people were all free. All of them. But how long can freedom last in this country? Not very long when you're living in this world. So of course we came along. We stole this country and look at this land now. It was bad enough to steal it, but we had to ruin it too. Now there is pollution, poverty, prisons, riots and killings. So much killing. It seem we can't live without violence and hatred. Hate!!! Hate!!! Hate???

How can you fight violence with violence? I feel this country has to be changed, and soon. The only thing is I don't think it should be done violently. I don't care if people burn banks as long as they don't hurt anyone. The only problem in this world is that people don't get along with each other." (Emily Marie).

*****

THE UNANIMOUS DECLARATION OF THE THIRTEEN UNITED STATES OF AMERICA

(Revised by Potassium Nacnud, Rep. of California.)

When in the course of human mistakes, it becomes necessary for the silent minority to dissolve their draft cards and political bands which have connected them with one another, and to assume among the powers of the Earth, like the Atomic bombs and Russia, the separate and equal station to which the Laws of Nature, of which are rapidly being polluted, and of Nature's God entitle them, a decent respect to the opinion of mankind requires that they should declare the causes which impel them to the separation of President Nixon and especially to Vice-President Agnew.

We hold these truths self-evident, that all men, except those different from us, are created equal, that they are endowed by their Creator with certain unalienable Rights, that among these are Life, Liberty, and the pursuit of Happiness, which, of course, will come later.___Now, to secure these rights, Governments are instituted among Men, deriving their just powers from the consent of the governed. If you don't understand that phrase talk to Mao about it.___That whenever any Form of Government becomes destructive of these ends, it is the Right of the People to alter or abolish it, and to institute new Government, laying its foundation on such principles and organizing its powers in such form, as to them shall seem most likely to effert their Safety and Happiness. But don't get any ideas buster, or they will put you in the pokey for being a traitor. Prudence, indeed, will dictate that Governments long established should not be changed for light and transient causes, such as electing the new, excuse me thats Ag-new, or forcing men to fight against other countries, or raising taxes to such an extent as to put everyone in the poor-house. OH, NO! They should be BIG problems in order to kick the government out on its ass. Now...uh lets see...ah yes! and accordingly all expenence hath shown that mankind was a fool ever to put hath in the dictionary at that time in history because anyone in this time will not know what hath means, so because of this mistake, mankind is disposed to suffer, suffer, suffer! Hee, hee, hee. But, when a long train of buses, excuse me thats abuses an usurpations, pursuing invariably the same Object evinces a design to reduce then under a strict diet, and plenty of pills. It is their right! It is their Duty! to throw the Government on its ass! and to provide new guards for their future security blankets.

We, THEREFORE, the Representatives of the united States of America, in General Congress, Assembled, SWEAR TO KILL ANYONE WHO STANDS IN OUR WAY! And to support this Declaration with a reliance on the Protection of Devine Providence, we mutually pledge to each other our _friend's_ Lives, our _friend's_ Fortunes, and our _friend's_ sacred Honor.

John Hancock
SINCE 1776   AMERICAN SAVINGS 5%

Jonnas Lyarrch	Butter Gunneth	Bruno Franklin
Arthur Dotenter	Lyman Stalk	Edward Rupertridge
Sammy Phozen	Geo. Walton	Step (Lightly) Hopkins
Wm. Parate	Garter Baraxo	Maxwellhouse Nixon
Tho. Slone	Gim Blooper	Spirit Ag-new
Joes. Commer	Bee Hives	Oliver Warhout
George Mythe	Richard Aston	Mother Goose
Granny Goose	John (Bic) Penn	Laura Stuttlers

Potassium Nacnud

*****

"There is a lot of poverty in this old sin-cursed world. Poverty is not only in Biafra, it is also in America. Thousands of people are starving. People are deprived of their rights when they lack what other families have. Its not their fault though. It makes my stomach turn when I see those hungry children. Some can't even cry because their stomach hurts too much. Their eyes become large and their bellies bloated. Their heads swell up. In America the poverty isn't all that bad, but its near it. In New York there are slums and ghettos. San Francisco and a lot more areas are getting worse.

When you speak of poverty some people don't even care because they have it good. But they don't. When you look at a person take a good long look and you will see that all people lack something. Poverty makes other people take up things that cost too much and are very expensive. Some starve themselves sick trying to lose weight. If they don't want all that weight they shouldn't be a pig and eat everything they see. Something has to be done about poverty." (Somon Marie).

*****

"As you know Democracy is not true. Because it is not taught in the school. Look where I live some people pay much higher rent than others. Do you know that the government makes a difference between the white people's welfare checks and the black people's welfare checks.?

I hear my mother and another lady talking about it. My mother don't have to clean white people's houses but she do and she found that the white lady she work for get $375 dollars every two weeks and a black person only get $110 dollars every two weeks with four children to feed." (Dude).

****

26. Assignment: In the year 2000 you will be about forty-five years old. What do you think life will be like then?

"I think that by the year 2000 either one of two changes will come about. Either the U.S. will become a strict police country or there will be much freedom. The way either of this will come about is that if people like SDS [Students for a Democratic Society] continue their violent demonstrations, the police will kill them and make very harsh laws, or the SDS will "win" and the country will continue on like it has for too long. I don't think these people (SDS) have enough discipline to run the country any better than those who are running it now.

By the same idea, the cops would run things so bad that someone, sometime would go. I don't know the answer to this that would work in this country." (Lief Erickson).

*****

"Date: sometime in May, 2000, place: a small midwestern town. At 6:30 a.m., Johnny Calle (a young scholar of nine) slowly opened his eyes and looked around the small shelter that encased his bed. He pushed the covers off himself and swung his legs to the metal floor (wood was very valuable and only used on jewelry). He put on his regular clothes (plastic of course) and checked the meter for the quality of the air outside his shelter in the house. Finding it excellent he took only one bottle of oxygen to help keep him alive. Thus prepared, he stepped into the air lock and waited. Slowly the air lock compartment filled with smog from the outside. When this was done, he dialed the combination and threw the two electric switches which opened the lock. Slowly, he pushed open the ten-inch steel door and stepped into the other room of the house. Johnny walked over to the closet and got out his (steel) school books, his protection suit, his light (for seeing through the smog) and his air tanks. He injected his morning food quota into his right arm, got into his suit, put on his air tanks, picked up his books and light, opened the air lock and closed it and opened it and stepped into the murky, brown atmosphere towards his school rocket." (Simon).

*****

"In the year 2000 I plan to live a happy life with my family. On a paradise earth. I plan to have many children in the year 2000. I will live in a big house with trees and flowers around it.

In the year 2000 there will be no more wars, no more fighting or dying. You can walk out of your house any time of night, not being afraid of anything. The life for me in the year 2000 will be very happy." (Shirley).

*****

"In year 2000 I know it would be a big change from what it is now. By then I probably will be married and have a family. It would be different cars, different buildings, everything would be different. I would probably have a good job. A nice car, some money. I would have a big home with a swimming pool." (Hal).

*****

"The sun tries to shine through the dense pollution of the smog covered sky but the suns rays can not exceed it. The people live in houses that have been built from the remains of the forests. Although there are many houses there aren't many people. The generations have ended almost because only one or two babies out of every five-hundred live. The rest aren't able to live in the environment that they have been brought into. The people are gradually dying off, for they are not even capable of living in their own environment. The once beautiful country has been totally corrupted by the most knowledgeable animal on the earth.

Food is very scare, it has to be grown inside special houses which protect it from the air. Water has to go through many processes which clean it. Air inside the houses has to be filtered first, and when you go outside you have to wear a gas mask, but "Standard Oil" still doesn't think there is a problem.

The suicide rate has g one up to 70 people out of every one-hundred, so that within seven years man, like every other animal, will become extinct!" (Emily Marie).

*****

"I read *Brave New World* and I didn't really follow it, but I guess I understand it in general. I can't just think of one general way the year 2000 will bring to us, but I have a couple of good ideas.

First of all, I think there's a good chance life won't be living in the year 2000 the way we're coining about our problems. Because we're using up the earth's natural re-sources, polluting the air and water, hating one another and so on. But if we just happen to survive it will probably be a weird new world. I think the population would be controlled by one or more people, we'd be governed very closely and we would probably learn in our sleep through wires tuned to our heads. We'd probably be taught the way the rulers would want us to know. Come to think of it the year 2000 is only 30 years away. I don't think it would be that controlled, probably just getting into that stage.... Of course, population would be controlled. It's a very confusing topic, it makes you think. In the year 2000 there probably wouldn't be any wildlife, sea life or anything living, including plants and we be making our own man-made oxygen, plants, food, metals, by then we could probably control the weather. Medical science could probably make our bodies live forever without growing old and wrinkled. About reproduction, it would be done in test tubes and experimented within the way people will act like in *Brave New World* that will probably really happen. Maybe in the future if we are ruled money won't take a place. We'd probably dig tunnels into the earth to get to China and stuff. By then we'll be flying to other planets and exploring.

But in general there is (I think) no way we can really survive because of bombs and wars and so many things. We can't possibly get by the great future." (Rabbit Paranoia).

*****

"I think that in the year 2000 that everybody will have perished from the earth or just on the verge of becoming extinct unless we have a revolution using whatever means necessary to get things done the right way and towards the benefit of the people not towards the enlargement of the wallets of the pigs in power." (Joe Fork).

*****

"So many people today are talking about the terrible future. I think these people are afraid of life. I feel that right now (1970) we, are at the height of the world's troubles and slowly through any means necessary people will live together, not to live afraid, but just to live." (Marie).

*****

"In April, 2094, during the hot and sunny part of the year, people were dying by the thousands. This happened because the layer of ozone, which is above the outer crust of the earth, had weakened thus letting harmful rays enter. These rays worked like a slow acting acid. Therefore, it affected everyone. The rays penetrated the skin and burned holes in the flesh. At times the rays varied. The people who had tender skin were affected differently. The rays were so powerful against their skin that the flesh was just eaten away. Other peoples skin peeled like a banana. The world was nearly dead." (Fritz the Cat).

*****

"The year 2000? I can just see it. Smog in the air so thick you can't see beyond. Pollution is everywhere. You are wearing a gas mask. The garbage is high. You're up to your neck in it. The bay is filled in. Where is it? Its gone!

The money hungry man will wipe us out with his factories that are causing smog. I will probably be living then and don't want to live in that kind of society.

Transportation will be almost the same except the cars will go faster, the jets much bigger, and the train much more powerful than before. All of this transportation helps the pollution get worse and worse.

The homes are going to be much more higher class and more expensive. People are not going to be able to live because the houses are so expensive and the food so much. Really believe me in the year 2000 this society will be fucked up.

The school system will be much more advanced. It will cost parents more taxes too. The children I think come out smarter than us because there will probably be better teachers in the school system. At least I hope so. The children who come out of this society will more advanced in the brain.

I personally do not want my kids growing up in a society like that. So, I think we better start changing it." (Ian).

*****

"I think schools will be probably on T.V. or something like that. Everyone will be on an individual thingy. And there won't be teachers, there will be supervisors. The kids will write down what he needs help in and put it in a slot then the T.V. screen in front of him will teach him just like a real, in the flesh, person. The kid will answer and it will continue. He can have a test on paper or oral tests or just about anything he wants. I don't know how they will do P.E. though.

That T.V. type learning will go on from 1st grade to forever, but they won't be considered grades because you will go at your own speed. If you don't want individual type learning, there will be classes with lots of people in them available.

Oh, I just decided what to do with P.E. It would not be good to have everyone by hisself all day so P.E. would be where they meet each other. It may not be the best place but it's somewhere. Also every other day there would be an all school assembly just to talk about things. Just like one large classroom. Seeing as you don't need as many teachers or supervisors, and seeing as there will be more people then, I don't know what they will do because there will be less job opportunities." (Karen).

*****

"In the year 2000 things will be much like today but more people will be dying and more will be committing crimes because they weren't able to get a job. Finally more people will be dying than being born. More diseases will probably sap up out of the hospitals, and people will die of those diseases.

In the year 2000 there will be another all out world war. It will destroy many many countries and people. The most powerful country will be Russia. That will conquer the world including the United States after great trouble.

Russia will probably join with China since they are communist too. England and America will try to fight back but, just barely won't make it, and then Russia and China will join with Cuba, and make the whole world communist. But finally China will want the world for themselves and so will Russia and Cuba. They will fight against each other. Cuba will be knocked out, and it will just be against China and Russia. While these wars go on America will join with Canada, Mexico and England. Those countries will conquer China and Russia and make them go capitalist.

After all those wars, over one billion and a half people were killed. Mostly young. In fact three-quarters of the young people of the world were killed. In the year 2052 there will only be one billion people left in the world, and, after a few more wars and atomic bombs, humans will be extinct, and animals will start to reappear by the thousands. And after about 50,000 years the Sun will burn out and the earth will be just another star in the sky. After a few time million years another star just like the sun will come in and time will repeat itself." (Jeffrey).

*****

"The year 2000 will probably be all machines, but we might not even be here by then. The world might look like a garbage dump, you will be able to see the fumes rising up. If people are around then, everything (just about) will be done for them by machines. These will be in all cities anything that is old will be discarded.

Things will be decided by someone else for you, you won't have anything to say about anything. You will be brain-washed.

People will live on the Moon and such planets that can be made livable. People will have little space ships to fly in instead of cars, and houses on earth will float around in the air, they will stay in one place though.

There could be world wide starvation, or all the poor people would eat (or the people who could get ahold of food) is pills. People will get water rations. Someone will figure out how to make water.

There will be a little jet pack that people can put on their backs and fly around. People will keep on trying to get ways of making transportation very fast. There will be all sorts of jet engine boats and supersonic jets.

I hope that the world won't be full of prejudice, but it most likely will.

Clothes will probably be all electrically lit up, with lights all over them. You might have to wear gas masks because the air will be so polluted. You might have to put pills in your water so when you drink it you won't get sick. Most likely every corner of the earth will be populated. The prices of everything will be very high.

We might even be at war all the time in 2000. Maybe people will be living under the water. People who have maids will have robots to do the work instead of hiring people. If you get a job, it will have to be from the government. The government owns everything.

Kids who go to school will be taught by computers or robots. They will be taught that the American Government is the best etc., etc. There will be the same subjects as now. Maybe kids will be taught in their sleep with little wires attached to their heads. There might be pills that make you learn. People might be made with all the knowledge that they will need, all stored in their brain. Instead of carrying binders around and writing with a pencil and paper, kids will carry little tape recorder things. They will record everything you say and -when you want it you just push a button and ask for it and it is played over for you. When you go to school you will have to wear uniforms. Every school will be just the same. Just about the only thing different will be school uniforms. Maybe by 2000 all the campuses will be very unrestful because of all the wars that the world will be in. Mr. Aston: Good luck in the year 2000." (Elsa).

*****

"In the year 1987 I was thirty years old. I was an airplane pilot. Every year I got three weeks off. By the time it was my time off things in the world looked pretty bad. The Russians were planning to attack America. So, I moved to Canada. When I got to Canada they were attacking America. All over the world countries were fighting. Except Canada because it was neutral. After ten years over nine-tenth of the world was dead. There was only five hundred people left. Luckily I was one of them. I was now forty-one years old. After a few more years, there were only twenty-one people. Twelve people walked on a time bomb and were killed. The others committed suicide except one. I felt that there were no living animals." (Jeffrey).

*****

"I think schools would be very much different. They will probably be computerized so that a teacher would not have to stand up there in the front of the room and teach you, a computer would. And it would be much longer, not from 8:30 to 3:00, but from 8:00 to 5:00. The computer would make you learn, and you would not be goofing off. You be saying, "Yes, Sir," and, "No, Sir." And the kids would be more smarter." (Pamela Marie).

*****

"In the year two thousand there will be no regimented "school." Learning will be free to all who wish it and want to learn. You will travel all over the world learning cultures and customs of other people. Participating in organizations and marches would be a way of learning. People would get away from the regular, dull, math, english, history, etc....and learn by doing, and in your preferred field.

You will not be faced with something you do not wish to learn about, for if you do not like it, you will just block it out of your mind anyway. Instead, you will learn things you think valuable to you and to others." (Vouix).

*****

"In the year 2000 we will all be dead. Maybe. As for schools, they'll be much bigger than they are. Everyone of every age will go to school at the same place. There will be a few gigantic buildings in each city, bigger than the biggest college or university. What a sight! Little tiny kiddies running around to their kindergarten classes. Minds of small children will be terribly advanced. Instead of having every grade level separate from the other, they will be all mixed. Kids will go to their classes. There will be people of all ages in the classrooms. The teachers will teach any one in the class at their own level. Also, some of the kids will learn things from their young adult classmates. They will learn quickly from each other as well as from the teachers.

The teachers will learn from the children and adults instead of always teaching them. Say, if some teachers are real up tight, I mean genuine old fogies who don't know worth a jive what's happening with everyone; suppose there's some problem that students are concerned with, or a cause, strike etc., they can get a rap session going in their classes and let them know.

All of the students will be completely united. Little boy comes up to a 21 year old classmate and discusses with him a list of demands or somethings. Everybody will be so together learning with and from each other. It will be practically the students running the school. On the outside it would look real innocent, though. Police would be stationed all over the campuses, not knowing why. And then one day the students will all come out, and with nobody on the outside knowing one bit about it, before hand, they will conquer the Capitalist society in one day." (New York, New York).

*****

"2000 Song
Taxi cab take you to the heliport
The heliport take you to the airport
The airport take you to the rocket port
The rocket port take you to:
Venus
    Saturn
        Mars." (Love Bug).

*****

"The year two thousand is going to be a very spacey year. That is it is going to be a year when many things are to deal with space ships, and space exploring. It will also change everything else like schools, education, housing, or land development, pollution and the general way of life.

In the year two thousand us humans are going to be changed considerably since the year 1970. Our language will change since we are all going to be one huge nation. It will be a language that each and every person can speak. There will be one supreme ruler who will rule each and every person. This person gets to be ruler by the decision of the people. All people will be at the same point of wealthyness, and will have his own job assigned by the government according to each person's ability. Each and every person in is on the world or any other planet is accounted for in the government files.

The schools and department of education will be totally changed from this period of time. Learning will be easier then since all the people have to be taught. A person wouldn't live if he didn't have an education. He wouldn't have a chance among all the civilized people.

Schools will be a very complex thing. The grounds will be extensive and the buildings huge. There will be many small classes, each class dealing with a different thing. A student will go to whichever class he wants to for however long he wants to. The teachers will be taken over by computers. In the year 2000 school will be fun to go to.

The population problem will be solve when half of the babies born in a year will be castrated. A law will be made noting that the most babies each couple can have is two. This ought to solve the population explosion problem." (Mark).

*****

"In the year 2000 all over the world there will be garbage all in people houses and in parks, schools, cities, zoo even, the rats will get a kick out of the garbage that will be hanging around. If we can't get kicked of that garbage by the year 1974, we will be living with the pig in their pig pen. Instead of the government building and tearing down stuff they should make ways to stop this garbage." (Stanley).

*****

"By 1984 to 1985 production had reached its peak. Some attempts had been made to stop pollution but the factory owners, car makers and drivers won their right to pollute. Education went on as it had been with a few new techniques here and there. They sent a few more ships to the moon. The last one crashed.

Marijuana was legalized and that brought some changes. For one reason or another the big companies couldn't get money out of it. Oh, they tried, and tried again and again but people didn't want to buy from them. They were content with waiting awhile for a friend to come back over the border or for their own little crops to come up. With the booming of legal grass came a few slight changes in peoples attitudes, but the changes would have occurred anyway only slower.

It had started along time ago and steadily it got stronger. People began to learn more and more about the parts of their minds that were forbidden. Even the smallest children began to study about the earth, plants, animals and waters.

Slowly and surely the youth began to seek simplicity. In communes and tribes and smaller groups they began to spread out over the unexploited areas of the globe. They were taught from books and experience and from those Indians who still remember the way. Soon almost all the young people had left the cities for the wilderness. Sure, there were older people who went but most of them stayed back and just quietly waited to die. All their children were gone. By 2000 there was no one under thirty (and a lot less people over 30) in the cities. By 2040 there were no people in the cities. They had all died either because the food ran out or they had nothing to live for. The cities had started to decompose.

The people made a point of forming no cities no matter how beautiful the area. Most tribes chose an area and learned that area moving nowhere else. There were a few tribes of nomads. The group chose a limit to the amount of people in a tribe allowed, according to the land. When a group had a certain amount over their limit some of the tribe would break off and start anew somewhere else.

The tribes lived in harmony and a universal law was peace. What had happened before 1984 was a reminder to keep all peace and ecology. If a few people from another tribe came they were accepted. Private property was known only in a few communities, that is, land, shelter and food, there still were some minor possessions that they kept.

As the races mixed the people traveled to different parts of the world before they stopped using vehicles to transport themselves. Prejudice began to disappear.

Most tribes had small gambling games no one lost much. It's man's nature to gamble and this fulfilled their need. Celebrations were held and these was usually consumption of some fermented drink or stoning plant and much music and dancing. Drugs were only used for the parties; they had no time for abuse.

By 2100 the cities had become overgrown they had not decomposed fully yet but someday they would be livable." (Adam).

*****

"In the year 2000 I think the world would be nothing but cats and dogs. They will be ruling the world. The cats and dogs will grow bigger and start eating people and killing little babies and little kids. And mothers that are going to have a baby. And old people that cannot help themselves. One thing is that I do not think I will be living in the year 2000." (Prudence).

*****

"Barbara gazed at the clock, counting the minutes until class was out. There was, unfortunately, only 1 hour and 45 minutes left. She put the finishing touches on her report just as Miss Edmonson rose to give the next assignment.

"All right students, time's up," the old lady said. "Hand your papers in please."

A murmur ran around the large, sunny room, and the papers were soon collected on Miss Edmonson's spacious desk.

"Now, if you will please open your *Viewing History* books to page 547 and read 'til page 625, I will let you out as soon as you're done." (This line of "business" of course, encouraged the kid to read faster.) The class smiled. Then one boy asked: "Do you want notes, Miss Eddie?" She smiled and shook her grey head. "Do you?" she asked. The kid grinned. She sat down and began to read the papers, smiled, and occasionally chuckled with mirth as she read the humorous lines.

Barbara, with some effort, took the large history book off the shelf, and lugged it over to her seat. On opening to the assigned page, she found the heading reading as follows :

"Chapter Fourteen"
"Life in the 20th Century"
It said that in 1982, the Population Explosion had really reached its peak. The housing problem was absolutely unbelievable. People were starving (to death) left and right. Inflation had reached such

a ridiculous state that people could hardly afford to live off their own income--most of them had to steal to survive.

A continental war was raging between the United States and Asia over a quantity of rice both countries claimed, and thousands were dying.

Animals, both domestic and wild, were dying off-from pollution-by the millions. Men had to wear masks in all the cities of any size, and it was almost as bad in the country. Water was becoming scarce and was so polluted that it had to be boiled a number of times before it was fit to drink. All natural, and even some artificial foods, had to be sterilized before they were fit for consumption.

Barbara believed this. Her mother had told her similar stories. (Her mother was in her mid-forties now, but she was only 26 in 1982.) Although she had lived in the remote country, her mother was still aware of the things that went on in the cities.

In 1983, the 30 year old mad scientist, Irving Samuels, developed a very harmful bacteria, and "let it loose" in a busy cafeteria of an important business firm in a large town just north of New York City. Once inside the body, it developed into an extremely contagious and deadly disease, which was passed on through any physical contact.

Of course it spread rapidly, as one can well imagine. Thus, the incurable disease decreased the world population from 65% to 70%. Irving Samuels, then made known the only cure (which he had developed long before he had decided to let the bacteria "loose"), and quietly killed off the bacteria. The remaining people all lived in remote areas—that, of course, is why they survived.

Barbara gazed out the window at the clear, blue sky, and then glanced around the large spacious room and at its 14 occupants. Her eyes took in the unmarred furniture, books, and other teaching aids, and she thought about her mother's junior high school. According to her mother's description it was crowded, and the students were disrespectful to the teachers (and the school).

She thought of her large, airy home in San Francisco and the other 70 similar homes on vast hilly estates, and compared them with the former sky-scrapers, slums, and smog of the city.

She also compared the old-fashioned open-air automobiles and their dirty exhaust with the ferry boats pulled by pulleys in underground rivers. There was a beautiful ferry stop at the bottom of her drive, with a lush three acre paddock next to it for people who lived too far away to stroll to the station, to put their horses in.

There were no telephone wires in sight because the phones were all wireless. Barbara pictured the ugly bulky phones of the 20th century and the slim, elegant phones of today. She looked down at her comfortable, sturdy, and pretty costume consisting of slacks of a soft yet strong material (rather like "broken-in" Levis), and the spring time shell she was wearing. They were pretty, comfortable, and stylish. She couldn't picture herself in the tight (and often embarrassing) mini-skirts of yesterday, nor in the bulky maxis of puffy, delicate blouses that were "in".

All the clothes anyone ever wore were designed to be comfortable and out-of-the-way.

Hair was another matter she thought badly handled in the 20 century. There were, she heard, great disputes about how long hair should be. She was glad that all the boys wore their medium long, and the girls all wore long hair. Her own hair was 27' long, worn in a braid.

She thought with pleasure how much better it was to have been born after the plague, and of the different changes she saw every year.

She looked up. Half the class had already left. She raised her hand. Miss Eddy smiled and nodded. Barbara left the room with pleased thoughts." (Eleanor Hume).

*****

"I have always had dreams that said that the world is going to be like a star space with beautiful sparkling homes and apartments all beautifully furnished and painted.

In my dreams I say it is going to be a perfect world with no war all peaceful, no pollution anywhere and the waters will be clean enough to swim in but you wouldn't want to drink it because it will be salted water.

We will get rid of the White racists, Uncle Tom's and them damned pigs that take advantage of the people.

Also having camp sites that everybody can afford. Everybody can be treated alike and fairly. Right on, World!" (Love Bug).

*****

"About three weeks ago I read a short book on Hiroshima, right after the atom bomb had been dropped. In this book were some gruesome stories of people dying right and left and people becoming deformed because of radiation.

Well, being so close to a major city in one of the most important states of the Union, I can't brush off the feeling of impending doom when a firecracker goes off down the block. Even though I have heard many reports about all our fantastic satellites keeping an eye on the communists and I hear about all our anti-ballistic missile bases, I still can't seem to get rid of my phobias of loud BARROOM'S during the night. Well, actually I'm not scared of every loud noise every night, just when my mind wanders.

But just think, what would you do if the whole city was being blown to smithereens and everybody was trying to split the scene before the fallout got to them. There's really not much considering the circumstances unless you owned a Boeing 747 in your back yard.

This is the big problem. What are you going to do in case a bomb drops? Run? That's what everyone will do. Hide? The radiation will find you. Kill yourself? Aha! There's the solution! But alas, I am a choosey fellow, now lets see...What to do in case of a bomb explosion?

I guess the thing to do is just leave the minute you feel it or hear it, just go. Most people (I hope) will hesitate and try and bring their things with them, but if you just hop in the car and tear off you just might make it. My guess as to the best place to go would be to the enemy.

But, seeing as that's very improbable, I would then go to the least densely populated area in America, like Alaska. But, also seeing transportation may be cut short, I would probably go to Sonoma or Mendocino. And if all else failed I would hide in a quiet safe and smelliest place—the s-e-w-e- r! sssshhhh don't let the commies hear you....sssshhhh don't let the commies hear you....sssshhhh don't let the commies hear you....sssshhhh don't let the commies hear you ....this tape will self decay in 2,000,000 years....sssshhhh don't let the commies hear you....yeah, me and my Winstons, yeah, me and my Winstons....sssshhhh don't let the commies hear you....ssssssss....BLAM!" (Potassium Nacnud).

*****

"Events of the Year 2000:

"Pan American announced first flight (non-stop) to all planets except Pluto.

We landed the first men on Pluto. After a grueling six years in a spaceship 150 men walked all over Pluto taking samples, pictures, and deep breaths of air, which is very strange seeing as this planet has no atmosphere.

It was decided early last year that the rather large star, "Alpha C", would be hollowed out to get an 9,876 square foot hole to hold a year's garbage pile which is 10,987 square feet of space garbage. Once done the star will be exploded.

Paris peace talks do not seem to be getting anywhere, but we're still proud that we could finally end the war in Vietnam in only 36 years, by no means a world record, but still something to be proud of.

The age long strike at San Francisco State College continued all year (again). Retired, acting principal Dr. S. I. Hayakawa stated shakingly; "I'll stick with it until I can do something for them." Hayakawa refuses to let them (the students) hire a new principal.

They stated: "We will get him to resign; if it takes a heart attack we will get him to resign."

Stocks: At the end of the year, elevators are up subways are down and envelopes are stationary." (Sir Genius).

****

27. Assignment: Mr. Aston's Report Card.

I am required to write a report card for each of you; why don't you write one about me?

"Mr. Aston can be
nice and can be
mean.
Sometimes he could
make you want to
scream.
Mr. Aston is an alright man,
and he teaches the
best he can." (Hal).

*****

"Richard Aston, as a teacher not of A-l quality. As a human being quite all right. He has allowed us extreme freedom this year, perhaps too much freedom. I'm afraid I've learned only a pinch of Social Studies and I'm sure in the whole year I could have learned more.

He could have taught us more, but as I over heard him say, quote, "I've been a little unsure of myself", unquote. He was, at the time definitely speaking about teaching at this school. I'm sure he is walking on unsafe ground. On the whole this year I feel I have been a little shafted.

I guess I like to be encouraged. I suppose I am so used to encouragement. I am not used to this. All my teachers up through the seventh grade spoiled me, pampered and encouraged me. Of course this year has prepared me for "high school and the rest of my life." I realize now (as I haven't before) that everyone-isn1t going to pamper me and be nice to me, but they did in former years, which isn't good to get used to.

I take it back. I have learned a lot. About China, "education-for-humanization-and-social-responsibility," how teachers and administrators work (think) etc., etc. Actually I suppose that this is even better than an academic education, and a lot easier to absorb." (Eleanor Hume).

*****

"Now let me see. You are a good friend to most students enemy to some and teacher to others. I remember when you first came everybody tried to think up a weird name for you. It took a couple of months to really get used to you.

I think you are a good teacher and you're really quiet, I really don't know why. Once in a while you'd tell us jokes or sea stories. I think you must make a good father, I don't know why, I just think you would.

Well, anyway, good luck next year." (Rabbit Paranoia).

*****

"You do plenty wrong and nothing that really interests me." (Henry).

*****

"Mr. Richard Aston is one of the best teacher I have ever had. He may not be one of my favorite teachers, but he is one of the best.

He has different ideas on the subject of teaching. He believes that a teacher is not there to teach, but to help the student learn. He has used this idea in many different ways. For instance, when he first came he taught us revolution by being a dictator. He has set up several types of individual programs, the subject of which the kids chose themselves.

This way of teaching is very good. It is much more interesting than being taught books. He has to do some book teaching, but not too much.

One of the problems with this is that the kids fail to be interested. They figure that if we're working individually they can get away with anything. I for one, feel like a fool. I sat around all year, not doing much in that class. So, this paper concludes my make up work and fulfills my assignments for this year." (Simon). When you first came everybody thought you were a super dictator teacher. Turned out you were just testing us to see if we went under our grievance procedure. This was really out-of-sight. Not many teachers would do something like this. Not many would ever think it is important.

Another thing is that you told it to us straight. You didn't jive around with how you felt; you told us. You seemed to be really concerned with what was going on.

I remember when you told you could have a lesson planned out for one day then, when you got to school, you changed it because you didn't like it. Most teachers would say to hell with it, and do the one they had worked on.

You don't seem to want to be an idol in the eyes of the students. You want to teach them." (Xathier X. Zeus).

*****

"He is about the only teacher who is human. He gets pissed-off, really bored etc. The other teachers laugh when they're mad and generally don't seem really human. If Mr. Aston is bored, you can tell." (Lief Erickson).

*****

"I like Mr. Aston because he is nice sometimes and he will help you if you need help on anything and he doesn't yell at you all the time. And when you go places with him he'll take a picture of you and he will play with you sometimes. But, when it comes down to business he don't jive a- round with you, he will be for real.

In the classroom when he tells you to do an assignment he don't mean for you to play around, and if you do he will tell you to go home.

Mr. Aston got a chart in his class to keep up on you. If you are not doing your work he will tell you is behind; and if you don't care he don't either. If you don't want to do his work he don't care. He believes in helping everybody." (Johnny).

*****

"At the beginning of the year, I was really dumb and didn't understand anything you were talking about or doing. But now, I sort of understand all this. As an academic teacher, you aren't really one, but as teaching other things, you're pretty good." (Valerie Valias).

*****

"Well in the beginning of the year I didn't like you at all, and I still don't because every day you always come to school mad and you take it out on us.

In the first place I don't think it is too cool because if you are having trouble at home you shouldn't always take it out on us. Anyway, you don't have any patience with kids so therefore you shouldn't be a teacher at all." (Kimberly).

*****

"As a teacher you're pretty good. I feel you ignore a lot of people, but you were just born cranky. You never speak to anyone first, they always have to be the first to talk. You don't teach very much, but I think I like it that way." (Maria).

*****

"I think Mr. Aston is a pretty good teacher. But, I think he ought to stick to the subject he is teaching and not go on to some other subject. He sometimes is not very nice. This is usually and almost all the time on Monday. I think this is because he feels he has better things to do and the weekends go too fast." (Jeffery).

*****

"Mr. Aston, I want to be really truthful about what I have to say. And here is how I want to say it. I have not learned too many things in most of my classes except yours.

You have taught us most of your knowledge but some people didn't catch on to what you were teaching. I think that I did, because when I told you I didn't like you I thought that you don't have to like a person for them to teach you something. I admit I was wrong and I'm very sorry I said that to you." (Somon Marie).

*****

"Mr. Aston, you really have been one of the best (well, really the best) teacher I have ever had. I like being able to come into class, sit down, and the assignment is on the board. I hate it when the teacher gets in front of the class and talks for half the period telling you what to do and you never have time to get anything done.

I like being able to write things down on paper. That is the best thing to do. To write things on paper when you are mad instead of taking it out on someone." (Emily Marie).

*****

"I really can't explain because my thoughts of you vary from time to time.
Sometimes I see you as a skinny bastard, but then other times I see you as a jolly, fat Santa Claus.

Today I see you as a shadow. You are over in a corner sorting papers and giving people dirty sneers." (Suzi Mantele).

*****

"I think you're a very good teacher and I've learned a lot from you. An awful lot of kids can't talk to you or explain things.

You're a lousy example for kids to follow. You drink and are sloppy and have learned a lot. You didn't go to high school so kids might think they don't have to go to high school. You might be a better person than a teacher." (Adam).

*****

"Associating with students: A.
Yelling at students: B.
Getting angry: A.
Cussing: F.
Controlling students: C.
Grading papers;:B.
Keeping up with work: C.
Sending home suspensions: A.
Teaching: C." (Tony Jackson).

******

"I want to thank you.
For what?

For letting me be myself.
I want to thank you,
for letting me learn.
I want to thank you,
for not letting me burn." (Little Green Man).

****

28. Assignment: Wednesday has been designated "Moratorium Day," What are your thoughts on this?

"Seeing that this is Tuesday, April 14, and more importantly the day before Moratorium Day, I am writing about something other than nothing for once!

Today at 10:30 we are having a couple of movies about Vietnam which happens to be a very important subject to me. One reason it is important to me is because I don't think America should be sending young men over to Vietnam to get killed. It's downright slaughter to do such a thing.

President Nixon could pull the forces out of Vietnam if he wanted to, but I guess he's afraid the Commies will use it as a base (South Vietnam) to bomb us or something.

The other reason is that in a few years I'll be old enough to get drafted and if I'm not in Canada by then I don't particularly want to fight in any war and get myself killed. I'd much rather die of old age or something painless.

The Moratorium, tomorrow in San Francisco, is a peaceful demonstration against the War. Unless the police get involved, the demonstration will be a peaceful one.........

As I am writing this sentence at this moment it is 4:05 in the afternoon on April 15 Today I hitch-hiked over to the Moratorium and I am now at my desk at home.

I thought the Moratorium was really beautiful. The. vibes there were really good. I enjoyed the rock groups that were there, especially Cleveland Wrecking Company and Country Joe and the Fish. But much more importantly I think was the expression of feeling about the war. I do wish Mayor Alioto could have been there so he could realize that there are people who realize what is happening in the world today. My parents don't know I went so I'd appreciate it if you didn't tell them at open-house." (Harry Bippo).

*****

"Today is Moratorium Day and I had to come to school, so I wore a black arm band to protest the killing and fighting over in Vietnam. We are supposed to write two pages that are due today so I'm going to write as much as I can on the war.

War is fighting and killing. People can't settle their differences by fighting. They only feel they can. When the war ends neither of the sides really win, both lose many things. They lose their homes and people, and they have their cities and schools to build again. They have to start new farms and businesses. Both sides lose in some way. One side may win liberty but that's about all.

Government sends men that are young to war even if they don't want to go. Even if the men have a wife and children they still have to go to war and kill others and others to kill him. Many men die before a war is over. Death is something that you can't repair after the war is over. Death of the soldiers--that's supposed to help the country. How does it help? Population? What could he have done if he was alive. He might of become a doctor or a teacher or a construction worker. He could have helped this country a lot if he was still alive, couldn't he?

A lot of people go around saying "peace on earth" but nothing happens. Anybody can say "Peace on Earth" but there is none. There's the war and the violence that happens in the cities. So what can "Peace on Earth" mean? I don't know. Can you define "Peace on Earth" and talk about the Earth truthfully? If you can, that will be a miracle I think." (Kat Hart).

*****

"I went to the Peace Rally in San Francisco. It was very crowded, there were hundreds of people all over. There were a lot of good bands and a lot of good speakers. I saw a whole bunch of people from my school. It was really a very peaceful rally, no fights or trouble. Although there was no trouble there was a large group of policemen marching in step. They each had a club. I think they felt like idiots. There were people all over giving out incense, which was kind of nice." (Sarah Richardson).

*****

"The cries of war echo, the bodies strewn across the battlefield. That is their grave, where they will stay; and be forgotten.

Beautiful lady, why do you weep? The country has taken your children to war. The babies you love with the labor pains you had. But still, they don't have the freedom to do what you want them to do. The law does though. The law can take the sons from your womb and send them out to die." (Emily Marie).

*****

"Mr. President,
You know that I'm against the war like everyone else. But, as you see, being against it won't help a thing. There are some facts that have to be discussed with the people. The so-called President and Vice-President aren't doing a thing. You're talking about bringing the troops out of Cambodia and you haven't done it yet.

You won't rule forever, so you'd had better get on your job. Cause it might turn out to be a woman's world in the next three years. If you know what I mean. Stop the war!" Peaceful Student."
(Somon Marie)

*****

"World War I
World War II
Vietnam War
What about World War III?
A purple hazy dawn
A fiery red sunset
And a beautiful day in between." (Janie).

*****

"I went to the Moratorium today. I didn't really like it because it seemed more like a rock concert. Everyone was really happy not mourning and I think the main reason most people came was so they could hear the music.

Nixon always has something more important to do instead of watching the marches. Past time it was a football game, this time it was the Apollo 13. That's something else about this country; we have to keep on until we kill someone and even if those men in the Apollo 13 get killed I doubt Nixon will stop the moon flights." (Emily Marie).

*****

"Kill," says the butcher.
"Kill," says the soldier.
"Kill," says the cowboy.
"Kill, "says the hunter.
"Peace," says youth.
-Silence-
"Bang," "Bang," "Bang," "Bang." (Rabbit Paranoia).

*****

"Why is there war? What is the purpose? What is the United States and Vietnam or any other country getting out of it besides killing each other? These questions are what people all over the world are asking themselves.

War is not something to be played with. How can you get Nixon or any other person like him to realize this? Do you know that the United States cannot go through one decade without being in a war? To me, this is a shame.

Here is a little poem I wrote about the war.
If you want I can tell,
about the war and how its hell.
Black and White brothers
Both do die
While Nixon sits on his behind. And lie." (Doris).

*****

"President Nixon said he was going to try and stop the war and all he did was withdraw 25,000 men and then all he is doing is moving more into Vietnam to make up for those he drew out.

I'm not blaming President Nixon for doing his job. I know all the men who live in the United States are fighting to save the United States and those who don't are fighting to save their country.

If any of you boys get called upon to go out and fight for your country I advise you not to fight and it will be easier on you. I know you won't like it but that's the way it is. Vietnam is strictly a killing ground.

All I can say is if there can be no peace in Vietnam then no matter where you go you will find no peace nowhere." (Edith).

*****

"I feel if people want peace they would have peace. You don't play with peace. What I really mean is that some people go around saying "peace," and when you turn around they might be fighting with someone." (Jake Brown)

*****

"Why does it have to be wars? People get killed, injured, and crippled for life. Why can't people live together in peace and be happy? Why do people have to live in violence?

If you ask these questions and expect to get an answer it would probably be power! Everyone wants power. Money power, political power, brain power, and power power.

Most people don't like you unless you have some kind of power. It could be the power to do nothing, but everyone has power." (Tony Jackson).

*****

"Well, I was at the labor march. It was full of old and young and long hair and short and worker and student, but they were talking peace, peace. Now kind of peace, old leftist kind of peace. It was a good feeling I got from the labor march.

When we got to the park near the Civic Center where we held the rallies the feeling of revolution grew. People were no longer saying, "We Shall Overcome" or "Peace, please," they were saying, "Stop The Oppression!". They were saying, "Power To Us!". They were saying, "Revolution Now!".

They were even saying, "Kill For Peace!". But the goal was not so much peace as revolution. These people don't know how to be revolutionaries yet. I think they were wrong.

So, what should be done? When is the time for a revolution? Which revolution? I truly believe that people would be a lot better off under communism. In a communism like Cuba (I shouldn't use it for an example all the time. What I mean is the idea I get of Cuba) where people are working for the whole not just themselves or not a big business. The more people work in a system like this the less they end up doing in the long run.

On the whole I didn't agree with the "revolutionaries." They were saying that they didn't want to work or assume any role in any society. You can't do that. All right, let's have a revolution. If you're going to have a revolution you have to have a cause. To stop oppression and poverty; now you have a cause. The second thing you need is something to give you the cause. Bring everybody up to the same level, the more people work for each other the higher that level gets; now you have your government. What are you going to do with it and how are you going to stop it?

Hey, you, big smart man, you tell me what makes you keep your government the way you formed it, or so that it isn't destroyed by a corrupt and future leader."

One of these nights you'll go to sleep (so will I) and when we wake "up we'll all be dead. 'Cause Uncle Sam will have pointed his last finger at the wrong Man, Country, Button and we'll all be blown to bits." (Adam).

*****

"Sadness fills my heart
I cry, and ask yet again
When will there be peace?
The sun shines softly,
Glowing orange-pinkish now
Setting, still shining.
Red blood, hate and gore,

Yet half the earth in slumber
Forgetting mankind.
Night, like a cool blanket,
soothing sores,
Oh, beautiful night,
Heal my wounds!
What is ugly in night?
Nothing. But with morning the ugliness
Hateful and loathing.
Beautiful night,
Ease my pains!
Now peace is around us,
Who would dream of hate? All is calm, peaceful,
Oh! beautiful night,
Drown my sorrows I
But during the day,
There is evil. Yet those who do wrong,
At night-rest
Oh, maternal night,
Give me sleep!
But tomorrow is yesterday,
The bombs will again fly,
Is there love anywhere?
Well, marvelous night,
Give me Death! (Eleanor Hume)

****

29. Assignment: The Flag

To honor the dead of the Vietnam war, the school assembly voted to lower the school flag to half-mast. This resulted in many arguments. Would you like to comment?

"President Nixon,

I am a student from Martin Luther King school in Sausalito, California. I am writing to you concerning the matter of lowering the American flag of our school.

I don't know if you have heard about the situation at our school or not, so I will explain it to you.

We would like to have our flag lowered to show our respect for the dying men, women and children in Vietnam (both American and Vietnamese).

The community and the board don't understand why we want this and won't let us do it. We have learned that to lower the flag we must have permission from you, so that is what we are trying to do, get permission from you.

Today at about 9:30 a.m. we had an all school assembly called by Mr. Walton (principal of our school). In this assembly Mr. Walton said that he was willing to lose his job, as principal, in order for us to get what we want and believe in, and that is lowering the flag to half- mast.

I think that if he is willing to lay his job on the line for what we want then you should at least answer our letters whether the answer is that we can lower the flag to half-mast or not.

Now the students of Martin Luther King School are in a very bad spot. We very much want to lower the flag, but we also don't want to lose Mr. Walton, because if we do we will be ruining the school for the students that come after us.

Please answer our letters soon.." (Janie).

******

"Last night when I went to the board meeting I was really surprised with how all the old people were talking. When I come home from school everything seems fine and I don't see much prejudicism at this school by the students. But last night all the white conservatives and a lot of the Black middle aged people were really showing racism and they think the school is the same way.

I think these old folks are too set in their ways and nothing can change their hate. Maybe they ought to go to school again and learn things the right way. Also, last night Mr. Walton was speaking about his views on things and was fired because of them. I guess that old ignorant board doesn't know that there is such a thing as "freedom of speech."

All I can say about that meeting last night was that it was terrible and frustrating, and I had to go home and cry to get the tension out because of the way people were acting.

About the flag thing. I think the board was making something really big out of something really small. All we were asking was to keep the flag at half-mast until we hear from President Nixon, and all these rich people from Sausalito act like it's the end of the world. I mean, Nixon has the letter and if he thought it very urgent he'd make a person-to-person call to Mr. Walton and tell him to raise it. But apparently he hasn't, and it doesn't look like anybody's getting hurt by it. If Mr. Walton definitely is out I'm just glad I'm not going to this school because there is going to be plenty of trouble just because of the old middle aged people." (Valerie Valias).

*****

"I feel very strong about some of the things that are happening in the news but most of all about what is going on in the mind of the reporter that comes to our school and hears the story that we tell him or her but when it comes out in the paper it is always a backwards lie and the same thing with the television reporters.

Every time that they come here and take a movie of what's going on and the kids it really blow their mind, they don't show that part. They show the part what they think people want to hear. They will never in their entire life show what really went down.

Martin Luther King's young teachers have got their minds together, the students have got their minds together, everybody at Martin Luther King has got their minds, all but these old teachers, these old good for nothings, all they can do for me is "   ". And I don't want Doggie [the school superintendent] to bring his no good butt up here either." (Puddingtang).

*****

"Last night I went to the Board meeting, and it was a bad meeting. Mr. Walton got up and spoke his piece. You couldn't hardly hear what he was saying because of all the people that was talking. One lady that was against Tolliver [the vice-principal] and Walton, was whispering something about the students in our school to another lady and I told her that I was a student from Martin Luther King and that if she had to say something for her to get up and say it so everybody could hear what she had to say. And what I think about them firing Mr. Walton is that if it had to do with putting the flag to half-mast we could have just put the flag up with no harm done. But now that they got rid of Mr. Walton they are now trying to get rid of Mr. Tolliver. And I think the School Board is crazy. Because I think if it wasn't for Mr. Walton we wouldn't have a school.

And I'm glad I'm leaving so I won't have to put up with Mr. Thompson. Year before last when Mr. Thompson was here he would let them get away with murder. Students, especially white, would get beat up every single day. Which I don't dig on very much. Teacher's purses would get stolen. My purse got stolen twice year before last. And I told Mr. Thompson, and he didn't even try to talk with the persons that were involved. I really don't care if Mr. Thompson comes up here or not because I won't be here to see him. I feel very strong about what is going on in the school and the lies that are going around about our principal and vice principal and especially about our school." (Little Green Man).

*****

"In the yard today, we saw a circle of about fifty black kids around Malcolm. Glen, the yard guard, came along and broke it up.

Malcolm walked off crying. All those fucking bitches went up and fussed and fucked and cooed and asked him if he was all right.

Walton called an assembly and was shit kickin' mad. He was mad 'cause he's busted his ass off trying to straighten us out, so's we can straighten the world out, and kids go and fuck it up. He said he wanted to be proud that "social responsibility and humanization" rang true in our school.

Now I know what happened to Malcolm will mar our reputation, but I also know he won't leave and that will help our reputation 'cos we're doing something so far-out a few punches don't mean shit!" (Adam).

*****

"MLK is a very good school.
I have been going to this school for about four years. And in them four years, I have seen a lot of things happening. Let me just sort of brief you on it. When I first came up here to this school. The principal was Mr. Thomson. Most of the kids like him because they can run over him.

He was O.K. I guess, but the kids just ran over him, they knew he was scared, so they took advantage of it. Mr. Thomson would try to be nice to the kids, but they kept on wanting more and more. He let them play records in the cafeteria. But then they wanted more. So, he had a Black Student union. Pretty soon he retired and went to be a principal at Manzanita with the little kids-something that he could handle.

So, Mr. Walton is our principal now. He is black and is also he is right on. The kids like him, because he take an interest in the kids. He laid down a lot of rules but kids still like him. Now they are trying to fire him. Who's they, the Board and the Superintendent." (Pamela Marie).

*****

"Why did they have to fire Mr. Walton? He is helping us, not them, so we, the students should do the hiring and firing. After all, what do they gain? We are getting the benefits of him and should tell the board or Mr. Walton if we want our principal or not.

I don't want a dumb dog for a principal. All he does is walk around with his hands in his pockets. He doesn't have our respect and won't get it. How can we learn under the eyes of a dull blob? Last year kids liked him because he wouldn't get them in trouble. That won't help us if we learn nothing new and never get chances to say what we feel. Why can't the students have a say in this? He is our principal." (Vouix).

*****

"I don't think this school would be worth coming to without Mr. Walton. The school would be nothing. The white man has tried for so long to get this school together, but it just hasn't worked. But this one black man can relate to black and white. Because he talks to us like we are adults. And he treats you like he would want us to treat him. He runs the school like it should be run. He doesn't take any jive from the kids; they respect him and he respects us. So why do the school board want to make some mess like firing Mr. Walton? Why? Do they have any kind of sense? Do they know that this school wouldn't be nothing without Mr. Walton. Do they just want to get rid of him because he is black? Why? Why?" (Shirley).

*****

"The Flag:
What's the matter with you?
Just what do you think you
stand for?
You ain't so hot.
You white, blue and scarlet lie.
Are you a symbol?
A symbol of what?
All that's good and true?
That's a lie!
I have been told

the stripes stand for battles." (Adam).

*****

"Ever since Mr. Walton came to this school the school has been much better. Before we did almost anything we wanted to. Now that he has come we are more disciplined than we were before.

I like Mr. Walton because we now get a voice in the school problems and in the school itself. Some of the kids don't like Mr. Walton but that's because he is trying to make this school have more discipline and the kids don't like to be disciplined so they don't like him. It will be hard for them when they go to Tam High School. Mr. Walton doesn't tolerate fighting, which is good and if you do fight you go home. Also, when you are in class and the teacher has problems with you, out you go. What I mean is that you go home and don't come back until your parents come and talk to either Mr. Walton or Mr. Toliver. After that you are allowed to come back to school.

So far this year I have only been sent home once and that was for fighting with a seventh grader. I just got suspended for a half-day. Mr. Walton came too late for us eighth graders but not too late for the other students." (Ian).

*****

"I am writing this little summary about my four years at M.L.K. I was here for 5th, 6th, 7th and 8th grade and I have had good years and bad. This is one of the good year because I have learned a lot more since Sid Walton has become principal here. He has tightened the rules and things have been much better than in my other three. In 5, 6, and 7 we had a principal named Thompson. The school was generally in a mess and there was no discipline. There were a lot of fights and a lot of racial languages.

Since Walton has come, there has been good vibes between black and white students and there have been very few fights. I think I have gotten much out of the 4 years I've been here because we are one of the few integrated schools and I have learned to communicate with blacks as well as people of my own race.

To me, I don't really notice the color of people's skin as long as they command respect from me, be they black or white. If I had gone to any other grammar school, through those four years, I don't think I possibly could have learned as much, not necessarily in the classroom, but out of it as well.

I'm really sad and sick that some people want Walton fired because he stood up for what he believed in. A lot of other people feel the same way in our school, including almost all the teachers. They fired him because he was a militant and he was black so draw your own conclusions of what America is like." (Harry Bippo).

*****

"I don't feel very good. I also don't want to write about the news because it doesn't make me feel very good. I think I'd better, though. Mr. Walton is the best principal I've known. Since he has just been fired, I don't know what is going to become of M.L.K. I have a feeling that all the people who are against Mr. Walton are really afraid of him. They're afraid of his success and afraid of black domination in our school. After a long time of complaining about kids being beat up and other such violence in this school, we get someone who clears it up and now they're trying to get rid of him. All the prejudice and racism is going to filter back. But I think Mr. Walton is a lot sharper, much farther along in his understanding of these situations, than any of the Board members." (New York, New York).

*****

"I'm going to write about how it feel about what's going on in the school. I feel horrible, if you really want to know. At night I dream of letters that I could write. All these people who are trying to mess up the school. Mess it up by getting rid of Mr. Walton, by taking away our freedom, by wanting us to be "good little girls and boys and do what the teacher says." But now I'm sick of it. All those people who try to do those things never went to school here. They don't know what it's like. But they think they do.

They think they know everything. They (the rich, high class Sausalito people, who don't have any kids here) think that by getting rid of Mr. Walton everything will be "just like it was before." It might but I doubt it. We have known what it's like to help run things, and hopefully next year's kids will try harder than we did. Hopefully they will fight for what we once had.

This year is the best year I've ever had here. The school set up was so much different, and I like it so much. But what was even better, what never would have happened with somebody like Thompson for principal, was how everybody is getting along together. I don't know about the other grades, but to me the eighth-grade kids are working together and really, really getting along. This is the best year I have had. I actually enjoyed coming to school. I have had fun this year. I know that next year when I go to Tam Hi, things will be very ,very different. There we won't have much say in what goes on, there we won't have any rights, hardly any privileges. But at least for one year here, I got an understanding of what it means to be able to get along with other people.

To read the news you would think the kids were fighting and rioting and demanding things and beating each other up all the time. But this is really exactly the opposite of what is happening. But because Mr. Walton tried something new, because he wanted people to help each other, and talk to each other and try to be friends with everyone, he was shot down. People kept fighting him. People are fighting him. Why? Because they are afraid. They are so afraid of how we might turn against them. Of how we might see something better, something entirely different than they have tried to make us like. Something that the whole world is waking up to. But they want to keep us blind. They want us to only see what they want us to see. That the blacks must stay in one world and the whites in another, races are also pushed into the corners of big cities. But these rich white people who don't know what it is like, don't want us to change anything. They like it as long as nobody bothers them about it." (Wildflower Weed).

*****

"So many things have been happening. Mr. Walton got fired and I know everyone at our school won't just sit on their asses and let it happen. I can say right now, that it's going to be so awful that the school will have to be closed down at least for a little while.

The people on the Board make me so sick. All they care about is getting rid of Mr. Walton (who was once a "full- time black militant") and they don't care one bit about the kids and their education.

It's supposed to be that they are to do everything they can so we can have the best education. Well they are doing the worst thing they could ever do.
I live in a dream sometimes,
Sometimes a nightmare,
Sometimes a beautiful fantasy,
But the beautiful ones
burst and fade away,
While the nightmares grow
Until that's all that is left,
A nightmare." (Emily Marie).

*****

"The Boycott:
When Paul Cohn said
Let's boycott tomorrow
Everyone agreed
Trying to show their sorrow
Yes, May 7 was the day
When Martin Luther King
Boycotted away
They thought it was wrong
To fire Mr. Walton
Now everyone going to stay home." (Tony Jackson).

*****

"M.L.K. School
Many years ago
The school was filled with strife
From chain gangs and greasers
'Twas a very stressing life
Then came the days
Of good fortune at last
The days of Richardson Bay
Where education came fast
Now the name's M.L.K.
And ill is our fame
Due to biased newspapers
Since Mr. Walton came
But it's just the opposite
Of what those newspapers say
Mr. Walton has changed us all
In a good sort of way." (Sir Genius).

*****

"I am gonna tell you my personal feelings about the school. I think that we're lucky to get Mr. Walton because we learned about how to get rid of teachers and how to strike and how to fight for your rights." (Stuart).

****

30. Assignment: The Grand Jury

In the past few months, a lot of criticism has been voiced about MLK. The San Francisco *Chronicle* reported:

> It has been five years since the little Sausalito School District strode forward from America's suburban communities and undertook the great educational reform of total integration.
>
> Today, the school system which was to be a model for the country is in disarray.
>
> The board of trustees has postponed its public meetings, pleading intimidation; the superintendent has resigned; the black principal he recommended has been fired; the chief school [MLK] has been closed after fighting among its young students.

Yesterday the Marin County Grand Jury published a report that is extremely critical of the Sausalito School District, and particularly Martin Luther King School.
The report states:

> What began as a beautiful dream of a fully integrated educational institution where children, regardless of social background, might mingle, work, play and learn together, has turned into a nightmare.

The Grand Jury lists as evidence:
1. Decline in attendance.
2. Financial condition and exorbitant cost per pupil.
3. Lack of competent management.
4. Lack of academic achievement.
5. Increased lack of confidence of the community.
6. Domination of Martin Luther King School by militants.

Comment on the above if you wish. You may see a copy of the complete report.

———

"Martin Luther King School is o.k. but it's the classes and the teachers. Some of the teachers is all right but some is mean. The problem at this school is that when you come to class they start hollering at you and writing your name on the board. They think they are doing something bad and trying to get you mad.

The classes I go to is alright--like room 9, 10, 12, art, home etc. The rest I don't like that much. But I guess I have to go to them. I dig how Mr. Walton has this school running. I like the way he got the Black and White together. This school is way better than last year. It seem like there was fights every day. But I know this school is together and I really dig it.

On April 14, somebody set the garbage can on fire and I don't think that was too cool. Last year they set the garbage cans on fire and all they did was cause a lot of mess. But I know I think this is a right-on school. This is my last year here, at least I think it is my last year here, but I will becoming up here to visit the teachers." (Ella).

*****

"M.L.K. School is a school of responsibility and rule that all students should follow. Some rules, like throwing rocks, and other rules and hitting someone with a rock could get a person suspended for a long time. But I don't agree with the suspended part because if a student gets sent home for something that he does it will just make the student mean and wouldn't be helping them get an education. If they are at school they can learn some more about life and education. While they are around their friends they can get what's happening around the school but while they are out of school they aren't learning nothing.

Some of my friends are very bad and show off they try to be bad, but they aren't bad. At lunch time I see lots of people throwing paper around anywhere on the school campus. I see some doing very bad things that could get themselves killed at the ages of 12, 13, 14, maybe even lower ages. Some of my friends be putting on a big front to be showing off in front of the white students, showing how much power they got making a fool of themselves for no reason at all that makes sense.

At the library students be playing when they should be working. Like it is the playing around and throwing their books around that isn't responsibility. They have to keep care of the school supplies for others next year and for the now instead of wasting them.." (Prudence).

*****

"I don't like the things that the Grand Jury report stated. Lots of it is untrue. Most of their ideas about how they think our school should be run make me sick to my stomach. It really disgusts me. Clearly they want us all to grow up Capitalists.

I have friends who go to different schools and when they tell me about them I find that I think this is the nicest school around. Here students are encouraged to speak their minds; there's much more freedom of speech." (New York, New York).

*****

"Years ago, when this school was built it probably was a beautiful school. But now look at it. It's in ruins. What I mean is that there is nothing to do around here. All we have to do is sit on the grass when it is not wet. Be sides, the benches we have nothing. What happened to all the record hops? And the time we played records at lunch-time?

Why can't we have some fun? It's just like a concentration camp here. When we do have something that deals with fun then some people in this school ruin it for others.

If we had something to occupy our minds there would not probably be so much trouble for people to get into. What do people expect if you don't have anything to do. Some, after a few years of nothing to do, turn out to be hostile, full of hatred and won't put their trust in anyone.

    This school will go to the dogs if something doesn't start coming up roses. When you think about it you don't even know what's to happen. Thats exactly how I feel. Things will probably soon change." (Somon Marie).

*****

"This school is like no school
I've ever been to before
The papers' writing about us
Now they're writing more
They are writing bad things
N'ope they ain't writing good
They're trying to get rid of us
Yep, I knew they would." (Tony Jackson)'

*****

"School is a wonderful thing
In school I get to
see a lot
hear a lot
say a lot
and this is a great opportunity
for me because I want to
walk with my head held high
in the future." (Love Bug).

*****

"M.L.K. is a school of love and hate and it may become integrate by all people in it. It is a school of social responsibility and when you come to a socially responsible school you must be prepared for all good things and bad things. You must be prepared for school and a lot of school involvement. You must follow the rules or you will go home because a socially responsible school must be handled in the best way possible for all students to get an education. We don't want any people that are going to make the school a bad school because them punks make it a bad school for all the rest of us. So, we just get sad at them people that mess us around like punching bags. Just walk all over them and don't even give a damn if they get an education or not. A school of love and hate, maybe become intergrate." (Prudence).

*****

"Martin Luther King School
Don't let the Grand Jury
Think they're running you
Like you are fools
King was always peace and cool and abided by the rules and rebelled to win the Nobel." (Roger).

*****

"This school makes me feel good sometimes, and sometimes it makes me feel bad. This school is right on to me. Can you see. Can you dig it." (Bettina).

*****

"Dear Members of the Grand Jury,
I am a member of the eighth grade at Martin Luther King School. I have read a copy of your report on the Sausalito School District and do not agree with many of the conclusions that you came to. Being a student at Martin Luther King School, I feel I should voice my opinions.

First of all, as I understood it, you studied mostly the year of 1968-69. I must admit, that was a pretty bad year, but still I got a lot out of it, mostly from my social science teacher, Mrs. Locastro.

The statement you said about Black Panther members in training allowed to wear the uniform is partially true. The most I saw was the beret, and some Black Panther buttons. Being a school where the students can wear what they want to wear as long as it does not interfere with another child's learning, I don't think much could be done. I also don't feel much should of been done. I don't think there is much reason why you should come down on Martin Luther King School in that incident.

You have stated that Mr. Walton said he was a full-time Black Revolutionary. This is true; but according to Webster's dictionary, revolutionary means:

> "Of, pertaining to, characterized by, or in the nature of revolution." Revolution means: "A fundamental change in political organization, or in a government or constitution; the overthrow or renunciation of one government or ruler, and the substitution of another, by the governed."

You have to admit, some sort of change must be made in the United States to give Blacks their rights, and Mr. Walton is a participant. Mr. Walton has a right to be a participant, and also think he still has the ability to run the school.

Your other attack on Mr. Walton which he said that Blacks will get their rights by any means possible. This is also true, but he also stated that his first resort will be a peaceful orderly way, and only in the last resort will he turn to violence. Didn't we get our independence from England using violence?

Your statement that many students are at the third grade reading level, among eighth graders, may be partially true, but let me list the literature books for all the eighth grade that we are reading. *Brave New World, The Yearling, Old Man and the Sea, The Pearl, The Autobiography of Malcom X, Animal Farm*, and other books at this level. Doesn't sound like third grade readers to me.

You attack Mr. Toliver, that he was doing the Vice Principal's work and wasn't credentialed. He may not be credentialed, but, as far as I'm. concerned, and I think I speak for many other students, he sure as hell is qualified.

Your statement that we should not give any jobs to people with any sort of prison record is just not right. Many people who have come out of prison have reformed and are good men. You shouldn't judge a person on what he has done in the past, but what he can do now. As Mr. Walton said when asked if we should not look back on what he has done, his reply was, if you keep looking back on what incidents have happened, I would also have to look back on what many White people have done to Black people. So you see, it's a two-way street.

You have said that, "What was once a beautiful dream is now a nightmare". Being a student here, I don't see many hints of a nightmare. I think M.L.K. is a damn good school.

When you spoke of the child who was transferred I think you are speaking of X. Even if I am wrong, I feel I should continue anyway. X did not want to be transferred out of M.L.K. You could say her parents forced her out. Now that she has been transferred, she feels that M.L.K. is a much better school than where she is at.

You spoke of the Free Huey posters in the office. It did not bother students as far as I know. I also feel that you could call this Freedom of the Press.

The Black Panther Paper in the library is a reality, but I do not think they should be taken out. This paper shows one of the many sides of a person's feelings." (Xathier X. Zeus).

*****

"Comments on the Grand Jury: I'm getting sick of the Grand Jury. They started with two facts and an assumption. They finished with two facts and they called the assumption a fact. Then they put in a bunch of fillers which are at least partly lies, and explanations, which are fake.

I know most of it is a lie, but it scares one that some people don't know that. It makes me sick that others might think it's the truth. I don't want to think about it. Maybe we can publically challenge each and every charge. I don't think they would hold up very well.

The grand jury started with two facts; reading scores are down and a lot of money is spent. They took the fact that there are blacks at the school, coupled with the black principal, and got the militancy charge.

They took prejudiced parents taking their kids out of an integrated school and charged the school with low attendance. I know it's not just prejudice, but a large part is.

I don't know about the money. I think I understand about the attendance. I know the militancy charge is penguin dung and the low reading scores I will explain.

This school has the lowest scores in reading tests in Marin. It also has the highest number of working class families. The families that have already educated their kids somewhat and put them into a school where everyone is white middle class like them almost will have better educated kids in the sense that they will write lily-white, middle-class papers, and will be able to do arithmetic. How much they will know about other people is another question.

Those who are put into school where there is not a culture barrier to break, where people write what they feel, and what they write is usually for real, perhaps can't read as well as some, but they will know about other people." (Washington Irving).

*****

School
is where you learn
the Golden Rule
They say ABC's is just like 1, 2, 3 This school is right on to me.
(Pamela Marie).

*****

"I remember someone telling me about a machine someone had invented that if you stuck it into walls or ancient ruins you could hear what a person had said at one time or another.

I bet, if you stuck that certain machine into these walls that you would hear sounds of happy people, people learning, people singing, people getting along, all types of people getting along.

I used to hate to come to school but now I look for ¬ward to it and maybe, someday, the people of the world may learn to unite, as we did." (Suzi Mantelle).

*****

"M.L.K. school is a right on thing.
It brings education and other things.
Newspapers, T.V. and radio men
They bring bad names and other things.
So, the newsmen forecast and other things,
but we know M.L.K. is doing its thing." (Check).

*****

"Now that I have the opportunity to write whatever I wish, I will take advantage of it.

The first thing I will write about is the most immediate thing on my mind about school. This is the Black movement. The Black movement, to me, is all right, its just what's happening in the school that's bothering me. This year it's better, but last year was terrible. It seemed like everything that was done last year was done for the Blacks. For instance: The school itself was named after Martin Luther King even though many famous Whites have died also. All the records played in the cafeteria at noontime were Soul. All history taught in school was Black history. Blacks got bus rides to and from school even though they were in a two block radius of the school, while other Whites who were in a two block radius didn't. Only Soul food lunches were sold in the cafeteria. Signs such as, "BLACK POWER," "BLACK IS BEAUTIFUL," "RIGHT ON BROTHER!" began appearing a- round the school, and many other noticeable things.

But, even though there were racial problems in the school, people would just treat the problems as problems. People seemed to try to ignore the fact that the Whites were getting beat up by Blacks. And even though people knew this was going on they still insisted the Blacks and Whites were getting along together. They even went so far as to print a book called, *Something Happening: A Portrait of the Sausalito School District,* which sort of gives you the impression that desegregation in the school isn't perfect, but it will be. That book is full of photographs that always just happen to be taken when people are on good terms.

And then, at school, if you look around the classroom you'll probably notice that the Blacks, and Whites, girls and boys are separated. Not by the teacher, but by themselves. This happens especially when there are tables instead of desks, like the library. Now if I were the one to be put in charge of getting the Blacks and Whites together, I don't know what I would do. But what has been done in classroom was this. The teacher came up to us and said, "Class, your parents are distressed at the way you have separated yourselves. Therefore, I'll tell you who you can sit with," etc., etc., etc. So, the parents and teachers got their way. The Blacks were sitting with the Whites. But instead of the Blacks and Whites socializing with each other, the whole affair resulted in loud shouts across the class which interrupted everyone.

Like I said, this year it's better, not much better, but it's better. Anyway, I have just given an over-all view, VERY over-all, (no detail).

BUT, before I close this article I must say one thing that's bothering me. Today in America, Blacks are making progress but, to me they are not really considered human. What I mean is, nowadays you see a Black on a T.V. commercial, in fact, almost every one on T.V. has one. But ten years ago this wouldn't be. It's like everyone is hiring a Negro just because he's extra special because he's fighting for his rights. I personally have seen very few people who treat a Black like a person. The rest just treat them extra special or extra mean.

Well, I've said what I wanted to say. Everything here I have seen for myself or on paper. None of it has been told to me by word of mouth. Everything is my opinion unless stated. The rest is what I have seen or read myself." (Anon).

*****

"M.L.K. school is a very good school to me. But some white people and black people do not think so. Some people think just because we throw rocks that M.L.K. is a bad school. How would you like to get wet? Because when it rains it makes a puddle, and if a bus can go around it why can't the old white people? They see you coming from school with your nice clean clothes on and they come up and slosh water on you and then start laughing. Before you know it you have a rock in your hand and hit the car. White and Black people do it. And if it was a white person they would do the same.

And another thing. White people think M.L.K. is a bad school because there are a lot of fights. To me all schools have fights. If they don't, then something is the matter with that school. M.L.K. is a school of black and white. But some schools you go to you see all white but not a black, not even a black spot." (Penny).

*****

"This school
has teachers
new and old
and students
different kinds
and different shades
And this
school
has books
and papers
And at
the far
end of
the tetherball
courts is
a tree
In this
School." (Adam).

*****

"The school is surrounded by a steel fence
Inside is the worn out
ground of a silent war.

Under bushes whites smoke
to the seeing eyes of blacks.
The whites get caught
and the blacks smile.
The next day someone
steals while another sees.
The one is caught and
Finds the one he sees.
The one who sees
doesn't come to school
for awhile
This shitty war where no one can keep quiet." (Anon).

*****

"There is a small place,
Surrounded by many big places
In the big place,
colors are different
In the small place,
colors are the same.
"Colors should be different," says
the big reading block from the
big places.
But the little place says colors
should be the same.
"Of course they should," the big places say striking back,
"But if they were, the stupid
darker colors would kill the
other colors."
"No they won't!" says the small place.
"Yes, they will, but don't tell them
that or else a lot of colors will be mad, just keep it cool."
"We believe in what we say," the small place says.

"You've been warned," says the big place." Your dreaded enemy, the *Independent Journal* will get you!" the big place says, and storms off." (Xathier X. Zeus).

*****

"School is a place where people come and learn. If you learned to stay in school you will know the golden rule. But if you don't learn to stay in school you will lose the gold rule." (Stanley).

*****

"Black and White together in
this school
Is this a dream or is it
for real
Are we going to stay together
in this school, Black and
White together.
It seems like they're coming
together
Will they stay together or
will they come apart
Nobody will know until
it happens or will it ever
happen." (Tamila Shalon).

*****

"How I Feel
The old, and angry
The new, and old
The good, and the bad
What's left beside
Love and hate
You love your friend
You hate your teacher
Why is it you hate your teacher
And love your friend
You think you're so cool

When you're nothing but a fool
Who can run around
and be so dumb." (Laverta Jean).

*****

"Our School
Full of beautiful things girls, teachers, grass, trees and even beautiful learning.
We even get something more beautiful black, white, Chinese, Japanese everything better than that, yes; homemaking, shop
It all adds up to what? Beautiful People!" (Jake Brown).

*****

"School is rule, School is cool, School is fun to me, School is neat, School is, fool." (Francis).

*****

"I think this is a wrong report and is a lot from last year. Things have changed since then.

This school is not a nightmare. I think it is a very good school where you have freedom to do anything you want and have a part in how it is run.

The jury gets mad because we are exposed to different cultures and ways, not pure icky stuff. They (I think) do not have any kids here or ever were here for a long time so they do not know what it is really like. They do not know how it has been this year. Things have gotten a lot better and they put last year's things in their report. That is not fair to write a report on things last year that are exaggerated about this year." (Vouix).

*****

"School: Sometimes a boring place to be But there's a good thing to see Not very interesting to me. But I go." (Jake Smoot).

*****

"Me at MLK.
One of many, but yet
Only one inside myself
Sort of confused by it

But not defeated
Walking around
Shooting the breeze
With all my friends
One of the grand (really guy)
But better than basketball!" (Harry Bippo).

*****

"This school is all right
But sometimes it gets
uptight.
The teachers are cool
That's why I like this
school." (Somon Marie).

*****

"A school in trouble, a school in turmoil '
This is my school
A school that is integrated a school that is free
This is my school
A school under attack
a school under fire
This is my school
A school burst apart
a school burst asunder
This is my school
This is my school and
I must help it ere it dies." (Simon).

*****

It is cool as ice water
It is cool as ice cream
It is cool as a boy
It is cool as a school
That's how M.L.K. is." (Penny).

*****

"M.L.K. for both black and white, most of the time there's a fight. People's opinions for this school, either it's all right, or it's out of sight. But that's O.K. because we're from M.L.K." (Henry).

*****

"School this year
Is very clear
We are going to do work
Without fear
Love or fuss
Kiss or cuss
This is our school
We can't get enough." (Tony Jackson).

*****

"Martin Luther King has a dream
for everyone to live and learn together.
Now our school is learning to get along.
Our school is an example for everyone, no matter.
We shall overcome." (Rabbit Paranoia).

*****

"A beautiful dream…has turned into a nightmare…" (The Grand Jury).

"Once a beautiful dream, Now a beautiful reality, Beautiful to those who will see, Ugly to those who will not." (Vouix).

*****

"To the Sausalito School board."
Dear Sirs:
We, the undersigned students of Martin Luther King School, feel that at this time the school is in the best shape it has ever been. The black and white relations are better than they have ever been. The students are responding to the teachers and administration. The words "education for humanization and social responsibility" really apply right now.

If you follow the advice of the Grand Jury you could really ruin the school. Please sirs, do not follow this advice and do not ruin the school.

Signed:

Alfreda Small	Dianna Tate	Lomia Booker
Allison Walker	Doria Lewis	Luan Fontes
Andrea Tasby	Doug Freedheim	Myrtle Ross
Anne Barnett	Erich Lathers	Nancy Sibbaluca
Barbara Giannecchini	Erika M. Hoyt	Peter Alvarado
Becky Cahoon	Frank Phillips	Philip Cohen
Becky West	Gale Jackson	Presita Curry
Belinda Triggs	Gary Andrews	Renee Lewis
Beverly Jones,	Glyntona Johnson	Richard Dawson
Billy Walter	Gwen Hall	Richard Kozak
Brian Rohan	Howard Turman	Robert Howe
Brian Times	John Wilkinson	Robin Hill,
Carl Schaniel	Judie Spigner	Ronald Ash
Chris Marrinan	Kathi McLemore	Scott Kresy
Cindy Long	Kathy Grant	Sherry Lewis
Dan Horowitz	Kevin Lowry	Stephen Dabner
Dana Mansfield	Laura Maresh	Sue Stump
Daniel Moore	Lee Kresy	Teddy Breece
David J. Robinson	Linda Allen	Tommy Tucker
Deborah Katz	Hollingsworth	Trellis Condra
Debra Williams	Linda Huff	
Diane Kamai	Linda Polk	

****

31. Return to Segregation

Following Sidney Walton's appointment to principal of MLK., at school board meetings white parents frequently alleged the school was "fostering black racism" and that "academic standards were deteriorating."

Charges and counter-charges were flung back and forth involving the principal, the school board, the superintendent of schools, community groups, teachers, students, and parents. The conflict even reached the international news.

The Mood of America, Sausalito, California

The middle-class white liberals of Sausalito, California, were proud of the integrated school where their own children could grow up side by side with black children of the nearby ghetto of Marin City. Then a black militant, Sidney Walton, was appointed principal of the local junior high school. He distributed his own book with an opening picture of himself, guerrilla-clad, pointing a gun over a pile of school books and captioned, "books or guns?" Faced with the realities of black power, white parents feared for their children. Walton was fired. Liberal school board members were forced to resign, parents withdrew children from school. A liberal showpiece experiment ended as racial confrontation, bringing to the surface deep, fundamental fears in the white middle-class community. The row goes on. The mood is one of tension and despair for the future. (*Radio Times,* 15 October 1970; BBC2TV, 21 October 1970.)

The result of this strife was a return to segregation. Martin Luther King School was renamed, and became a "white" school, while a school, with the name Martin Luther King, was opened in "black" Marin City).

In 2013, years after most American school had been integrated, the Martin County Grand Jury ordered Sausalito to desegregate their schools, thus, hopefully, ending forty-three years of apartheid.

THIS SCHOOL,

WAS LIKE A TRIP,

TO HAPPY LAND!

(Stanley)

PART TWO

AGNEWS STATE HOSPITAL
AGNEWS, CALIFORNIA

Introduction

California law mandates that all children, from six to eighteen, receive an education. For those unable to attend a normal school, educational services still must be provided, this includes those detained for some reason in a State facility. In 1971 I was employed by the State of California as a "Special Education Teacher," and assigned to a hospital.

Agnews State Hospital, formerly called Agnews Insane Asylum, was [it is now a business park], an hour's drive south of San Francisco. A scatter of low-rise buildings in a garden-like setting, it had a pleasant atmosphere, with the school a short walk from the residential wards.

On the first morning of class, eight teenage students were escorted into the classroom by an attendant. He explained that he was a "psych-tec" and would always be near if needed. The students sat, slumped in their seats, seemingly in a daze. When I said, "good morning," there was only a mumbled response. After I had taken the roll, one boy, Jimmy, spoke up.

"You're new here, aren't you? First thing for you to know is we've just had our morning dose of Thorazine, which makes you kind of dopey, we'll get a bit livelier later, so let me let me tell you the score. Agnews is divided between the "tards" [retarded] and the "crazies." We are the "crazies," you won't ever see the "tards." You wouldn't want to. Sometimes the psych-tecs in charge of us let us sneak a look at the tards. You wouldn't believe it. Old men and women in cribs, just wearing diapers. Some of them all deformed. They've even got one with two heads. I get nightmares about that place."

He continued, "We crazies are divided into the real nuts that are locked up all the time, and us, the part-time crazies. We are usually o.k. They keep us stoked up on Thorazine, which sometimes make you feel like the walking dead. The psych-tecs are supposed to watch you swallow your dose, but occasionally you fake it 'cos you just want to feel half normal. The psych-tecs rule the place, if you act-up they tell the shrink, who increases your dose, or even puts you in a locked ward. On the other hand, if you play it right, you can come here to class, use the gym and the library, and have some free time."

The 5150's

A few days later, Jimmy gave me insight to the student's view of their situation. "Another term for us is a "Fifty-one fifty," that's a legal term for someone who is danger to themselves, or others, and so can be held in protective custody. However, I know that a minor 5150 must be released on their eighteenth birthday, so in a few months you can bet I'll be out of here."

Though weekly meetings with the student's "shrink," and the other teachers, we all learned something of the student's past, however, for many patients, memories of past were too painful for them to talk about them. Often, lashing out at others, or self-harm, was the only way to obscure memories of past events. Spending six hours a day, five days a week, with the students sometimes established an understanding that their monthly, one hour session, with a psychiatrist did not.

Frequently, it was from students that we learned of the problems faced by the others. Such as, "Reggie blew up last night, his girlfriend hadn't written to him, he was depressed, and hadn't been swallowing his meds. He just lost it, raving and banging his head against the wall. So, he's confined to the ward for a while." Or, in another case, "Mary found a piece of glass and started cutting herself again—she's in the hospital for a few days."

Parents

While discussing a particular case during staff meeting, often someone would mutter, "crazy child, crazy parents." A few examples.

Ronnie was an athletic boy, who had even run in the 1970 Special Olympics at Chicago. For long periods he led a normal life, but then he was hit by severe depression and thoughts of suicide. Regular medication prevented these episodes. However, his father did not believe in "drugging" his son. So, there evolved a cycle of Ronnie being admitted, released after a short stay, then, a month or so later, back again after another incident of self-harm.

Steven, was a highly intelligent boy, capable of doing math that even his math teacher had difficulty in following. He was friendly and outgoing, so it was hard to see why he was being held. One incident gave a clue.

Another teacher and I had taken a group of student to the hospital's library where they could borrow books. While there, the teacher whispered, "You see that woman checking out books? That's Steven's mother. She volunteers here, but she never even looks at her son, and he ignores her. It's really strange." That afternoon, when the students returned from lunch, Steven came in carrying a live pigeon, as he sat down he ripped its head off with his teeth and squeezed the blood all over his desk. The psych-tech took Steven back to the ward and the next day he came back to class his normal, friendly, self.

Jane was the saddest case. At the age of thirteen she had given birth. The man responsible for her pregnancy was unknown but suspected of being her brother or father. [In an age before DNA, there was no way of telling.] A short time later she put the baby into a hot frying pan.

At Agnews she came to class regularly, although she seldom spoke. Incidents of self-harm were frequent. She would tear at her arms with her teeth until the blood was running or cut other parts of her body.

The Students

The classes ranged widely in age, academic ability, and personality. A couple of students were extremely withdrawn while others, like Jimmy, were very self-assured and outspoken.

Ralph was strangest case; his conversation constantly included the words "vacuum cleaners." Such as, "My mother has lots of vacuum cleaners." Or "Do you have any vacuum cleaners.?" Sometimes "vacuum cleaners seemed to refer to cigarettes, as in, "My father smokes a lot of vacuum cleaners," but then he might ask, "How many vacuum cleaners are on a bus?" In doing school work Ralph was quite competent, able to participate in discussions, but every once in a while would mutter "vacuum cleaners," which the class ignored.

George was hard to assess. He had only been in the class for two days when I took them to the craft shop, where the patients could participate in various activities, which might involve scissors, knives, or screwdrivers. Having not yet received Georges file, all I knew about his was that he had stabbed his mother to death. With this knowledge in the back of my mind, I was shocked when, out of the corner of my eye, I saw George walk behind me, then I felt a hard jab in my back. As I spun around I realized it had only been his thumb. Then both of us, realizing what the other was thinking, burst out laughing. For the rest of the time, he was in the class, George appeared to be an easy-going, normal, teen-ager never giving a clue as to what sparked his hatred for his mother.

Several times we took a group of students off campus to a museum or a park. On these excursions a different atmosphere prevailed, almost of happiness; while being pushed on a swing, even Jane laughed.

An incident demonstrated that, in one respect, they were normal teenagers. One day, as the shrink left for the day, he found a group near his car, giggling and pointing to one of the wheels.. The hub cap was gone, as were the lug-nuts that held the wheel in place. Pondering what to do, he said, "I guess I'll have to call the car company to bring out some replacements." Whereupon, Jimmy, the obvious ring-leader, advised, "Why don't you take one nut from each of the other wheels and put them on that wheel, that way you can drive home." When the shrink replied, "That's a great idea." Jimmy retorted, "We may be crazy, but we ain't stupid!"

Closure

Several force resulted in the closure of Agnews 5150 unit. When Ronald Reagan became governor of California in 1967, and again in 1971, he initiated a program of privatization, allowing for-profit companies to take over the functions of state organizations. This move was supported by a segment of the public, particularly a group of upper-class people, who after an accidental overdose, had been found 5150 and confined to an asylum. Now they were able to do their time in a comfortable, country-club, setting.

The less fortunate, particularly the juveniles, were palmed off to privately owned businesses termed, "Residential Treatment Homes." There, their "treatment" consisted solely of tranquilizing drugs, and their education limited to a once a week visit by a teacher who simply handed out work-sheets. With little support and supervision, many patients walked out, starting a cycle of detention and homelessness that often ended on the sidewalk or in the morgue.

******

One morning, shortly before the closure of Agnews juvenile wards, one of the students asked, "Did you hear about Jimmy? Two days ago, he was eighteen, he just walked out. He hitch-hiked to the airport where he found a post-office truck with the engine running. He got it into gear, then drove down the run-way trying to take off. He crashed at the end, but wasn't hurt. So he's 5150 again, but this time as an adult."

******

Moving on

After Agnews closed I was still employed by the State of California and shuffled around other juvenile detention centers as a temporary substitute for the permanent teachers. These classes could be at those 5150 facilities yet to be closed, or the California Youth Authority (CYA) correctional centers, for minors convicted of committing crimes.

The atmosphere at these could vary greatly, from grim to apparently pleasant. At one, the boys showed me the blood splattered walls of the elevator, which, they claimed, was routinely stopped between floors, so an inmate "could be taught a lesson." Yet, at another, I was told, "This place is great, you get a bed of your own, you can watch T.V. all day, and even smoke. The best thing is they give you onions on your hamburger."

PART THREE

OAKLAND UNIFIED SCHOOL DISTRICT, OAKLAND, CALIFORNIA

The Setting

Oakland School District, across the bay from San Francisco, provides an education for fifty-thousand children, of these seven-thousand have "special needs." These can be of a number of kinds, from having a physical disability to being on remand in juvenile hall.

A large portion of "Special Ed." students fall into the category of "Emotionally Disabled,"(E.D.), or "Emotionally Handicapped," (E.H). This means they are, "unable to build or maintain satisfactory interpersonal relationships with peers and teachers." In practice, this covered a wide range of behavior from being withdrawn to very aggressive — often in the same student.

In 1977, after a probationary period of moving around the school district, I was given a permanent assignment. Was I lucky! Most E.D. classes were housed in small, mobile home like, "portables," containing eight, shoulder-to-shoulder, student carrels, , and a teacher's desk, and as far from the main school building as possible. Instead, I was assigned what had been a wood-shop. A large building divided into a work area (the benches, and the tools still there) and, separated by a glass wall, a normal classroom. Furthermore, there was a toilet. This meant there was no need to write hall passes for students to go the distant facilities, from which they might return hours later, if at all.

Best of all, I was given a teaching assistant, a recent Indian immigrant, who spoke better English than me, and had previously been a school principal. With a class of only eight students, this meant we were able to give more individual attention than they would normally receive.

Using both the classroom and the work-benches, it was possible to separate the students while they were working on individual assignments. This was great advantage, as there were always some who could work quietly by themselves, while others were restless and sometimes disruptive.

The Students

While all my students had been labelled "Emotionally Disabled," no two were alike. Gerald seldom spoke. He could ask, or answer a question, but always in as few words as possible. In reading and writing he was quite competent, but he just could not read aloud, or participate in a class discussion.

Jenny was the exact opposite. A small girl, she was in constant motion, squirming in her chair, always happy, and almost a non-stop talker.

Willie was boiling over with anger, uncontrollable, he frequently got into fights with other students, and cut class. The first major incident was when he turned up in the school yard with a shot gun and started firing at random. [The judge told him "Be a good boy and don't do it again.].

The wood-shop, where I held classes, was quite spacious, so I allowed students to keep their bikes there, provided they brought them in before school and took them out after school. One day, after I hadn't seen Willie for days, he walked in and tried to take a bike. When I stopped him, he lashed out, hitting me in the face. When he saw the blood running down my face and dripping off my chin, he ran. [Once again, the judge told him to be a good boy and not to do it again.]

[I never saw Willie again, but I did hear of him. A few months later he broke into an old woman's house and tried to rape her. She managed to call the police. When they arrived, Willie started shooting at them. Luckily, he only had a few shot-gun shells, and surrendered before anyone was injured. A year or so later, I heard he had been charged with murder in an unrelated incident.]

The Lives of "Children"

During a unit on economics, while the class was discussing wages and income, a boy proudly said he made twenty-five dollars a week delivering newspapers. On hearing this, a girl burst out laughing, "Twenty-five a week? That's nothing, I make fifty a night

This, was hard to believe, as Ellie came to class every morning bright, alert, and cheerful. However, late one night, as I was driving home from a party, down a boulevard noted for its street-walkers, there was Ellie, with other girls, flagging down cars.

*****

Janine was a good looking, sexually provocative girl, who seldom turned up for class. After being absent for a week, she showed up one mid-morning. When I asked why she hadn't been in school, she replied, "The cops picked me up, claiming I was soliciting, and took me to Juvi (Juvenile Hall Detention). But, did I get back on them. I peed in the back of their car."

*****

Michael had not been to class for over a month when, one morning, he strutted into class. "You chumps still here? You ought to come work for me. Look," he says, pointing though the open door, "That's my Caddy and driver—got to have him because I'm too young to drive. But, see here" he says, lifting up his shirt and proudly pointed to bullet wound in his side, "I'm in the big time!"

*****

Frequently, boys would bang on the classroom door, demanding to speak to Doris. I didn't understand her popularity until the day she walked into class carrying a baby, face down, under one arm, while she sucked on a lollipop. Proudly, she said, "I want to show the kid to my friends, its eighteen months old, and now I'm pregnant again." [Doris was thirteen.]

*****

The home life of many students was often, to put it mildly, not conducive to learning. Steven was often absent; when I asked why, he replied that he loved to paint, using oil paints, which were expensive, so he had a part-time job in a grocery store. Sensing something was not quite right, I decided to make a home visit and drove him home one afternoon. Entering the house, we found his mother sprawled on a couch, crack-pipe in hand, barely conscious. When I asked Steven if we should call an ambulance. As he gently wiped her mouth, he said it was o.k., and that he knew what to do.

*****

The situations that many students experienced were often traumatic, yet, outwardly, often treated lightly.

*****

"Mr. Aston, guess what. Last night my mom and Lenny's mom, got into an argument. I don't what it was about, but they started up shooting at each other across the courtyard. Lucky for them, no one got hurt."

*****

Another morning, Mary, usually a lively girl, came into class and put her head down on the desk. When I asked if she was okay she replied. "Last night my sister and her boyfriend had an argument. He pulled out a gun and shot her. She crawled into the bedroom, he followed and finished her off. So, I don't feel like doing math this morning."

*****

Annie, was small for her age, yet full of life, and always happy, yet her response to this incident, was dis-quieting.

"Last night, my mom and her boyfriend got into an argument, and he threw the T.V. out the window. So she grabbed a kitchen knife and stabbed him in the neck. The blood shot up right to the ceiling." "And that," said Annie, slapping her desk, "Was the funniest thing I've seen in my whole life!"

The student's, and the parent's attitude toward education was often unexpected.

******

"I can't do any work this period, my fingernail polish ain't dry.

*****

"I couldn't do the homework co's I was watching T.V."

*****

"You'd better not mark me tardy—I got up late-you just ask my mother."

*****

"I was absent last week because Tuesday night I started baby-sitting for our neighbor, but she didn't come home till Friday."

*****

When a parent was told her twelve year old son frequently cut class, she replied, "He pays the rent [by selling dope]," so I can't tell him what to do."

*****

On calling a mother to tell her that her son had tried to stab me, she was furious. "I've been looking all over for that knife, you tell him to bring it home right now."

*****

Once upon a time, it was common for teachers to reprimand students by having them stay after class to complete an assignment. The first, and only, time I tried that, I was told, "You make me stay late, I will tell everyone you tried to rape me."

Teachers seldom get to know anything of a child's life outside of the school setting, and its effect on the student's behavior. Only in a few instances are a probable causes suggested.

*****

Ronnie loved airplanes, particularly the Lockheed L-10-11 Tri-Star. Given any hint of interest, he would reel off a long list of its specifications—top speed, engine thrust, passenger capacity—and more.

Once came to class with photos of him sitting at the controls of an airliner. Asked how he got them he replied, "It's easy. I wait just outside the exit gate until I see passengers coming out. Then, yelling "I left my in the seat pocket!" I run in, pass the attendant. Once on board, I get the clean-up crew to take my picture."

Over time, Ronnie's comments grew darker, starting with such questions as, "What would happen if I threw a brick into the engine while the fan is still spinning? Eventually, he was repeatedly saying, "We live right under the airport flight path. One day I'm going to shoot a plane down with my Daddy's shot gun."

Ronnie's change of mood seemed strange until one day, his family came in for a meeting with the guidance counselor. During the conference, only the father, in military uniform, spoke; while the mother and son sat, with heads bowed, looking at the floor. As they were ready to leave, the father stood, barking, "Attention! Left-face! Quick-march!" As the family trooped out, I gained some understanding of Ronnie's misplaced hostility.

*****

Gerald was an able student. He worked well above grade level, however, he was subject to outbursts of anger, frequently lashing out at other students, and initiating fights. Only through a meeting with Child Protective Services, did I learn, for years, his mother had forced him to submit to the sexual abuses of her boyfriend, by burning the boy with cigarettes if he rebelled.

*****

Arthur's personal devils were unknown. Constantly withdrawn, he seldom showed any emotions, so this incident shocked the whole school. One day after school, a teacher saw him riding down the street on his bicycle. Hanging from the handlebars was a clear plastic bag. In it, quite visible, was a human foot.

Arthur told the story to the police without any apparent emotion. One day after school, he and a friend got into fight. Picking up a brick, he killed the boy, dragged the body into a near-by vacant house, and sawed the body into parts. Piece by piece he carried these down to Oakland harbor and threw them into the Bay.

As he put it, "I'm smart. To fool the cop, I painted the toenails red—so they would think it was a girl."

―――――――

Violence in Schools
Although the student's view of the world, and indeed their lives, must be influenced by daily events, few mention it in their writing. In many schools, violence is endemic, with rarely a day passing without an incident. A few examples from my journal:

*****

Last evening, in the gym locker room, a boy, there for basketball practice, was shot dead. This is not the first killing on school grounds. There has been innumerable violent incidents, many involving firearms. Several students, and one policeman, have been murdered at just this one school.

*****

An ambulance came three times today, as there is trouble between black and Hispanic gangs. When school let out, a police car was stationed on each corner of the school block, with police officers holding shotguns.

*****

"Gang-bangers," with Uzi machine pistols, have been spraying local houses at random. One woman told reporters her kids sleep in the bath tub as protection from stray bullets. It is not unusual for the police to find forty, or fifty hits, on a single house, with shell casings scattered on the street. "However," said a police spokesperson, "people are not often injured, with the shootings so commonplace residents do not bother to report them anymore."

―――――――

In many students, anger and hostility constantly roil beneath the surface, ready to explode in verbal abuse, shoving and hitting.

*****

Every day the same students are cutting class. Last Friday, during 6th period, fifteen students were playing around in the main hall, while upstairs others were dragging the fire hoses out of the cabinets. These were the same students who have been openly gambling all year, and who were setting off firecrackers last week. All the kids have got the message that nothing will happen to them. Last week, the campus control officer quit in disgust, because the administration will take no action. Many times I have heard an administrator say to a passing student, "You are on suspension, and not supposed to be on campus," — then kept on walking. (Journal)

*****

Meanwhile, teachers dare not put a hand on a student, even to stop a fight, for danger of being accused of molestation.

Despite this constant violence, the California Supreme Court ruled that disruptive students cannot be expelled from school. In a case concerning a boy who had tried to choke a girl, and smashed classroom windows — for which he was duly expelled. His parents sued the school, winning damages of $40,000. Subsequently, the Court ruled the boy was entitled to stay in school because he was crazy, and therefore not responsible for his actions.

In another case, the mother of a student, who was shot dead by a classmate, sued the school district for failing to provide a safe environment. Yet, the Court has also ruled it is illegal for school staff to search a student's person, book-bag, or locker. Consequently, this year all lockers are permanently locked — because of all the drugs and weapons previously found in them.

School's Out

The school year is 180 days, however few, if any, of my students were present every day. Consequently, my knowledge of their lives was minimal. At the best of times, teen-agers have difficulty coping with their emotions, but so many of those I met lived under exceptionally difficult conditions. What I did learn, the more saddened I became that so many were caught in a world over which they had no control.

Of all the many hundred students I had the privilege to meet, I know nothing of their later lives, and often wondered if I made any difference. Only two called me, years after they had moved on: one to say he was now in the army; the other to tell me of his job.

At two o/clock one morning my phone rang. It was Ronnie, the boy who loved airplanes. "Mr. Aston, I wanted to say hello." "At this time of night? "I'm on my break." "What do you mean. 'On your break"?" "I work the at the airport. I'm part of the maintenance that service planes between flights. I thought you would like to know I made it."

AFTERWORD

The Death of Literacy

One day, in 1986, I walked into the school library and found the Principal and Librarian plucking books from the shelves--books with such titles as, "*Huckleberry Finn*," "*To Kill a Mocking Bird*," and "*Ann of Green Gables*"-- and packing them into boxes. The Principal explained, "Kids don't read books anymore, so we are packing these off to the district depository, so as to make room for computers." It turned out that only a few high-school teachers knew anything about computers, so the machines destined for junior high-schools sat for years in the district warehouse, gathering dust while the books were "recycled."

Over the years, large table-top computers morphed into tablets, then to cell phones, with most public schools financially unable keep pace with developments. The cost of home computers, and the later personal communication devices, started to widen the literacy gap between students.

At present, according to various sources, the U.S. is thirty-sixth, [or, by some accounts even sixtieth] in world literacy rankings, certainly below that of Russia, China, Iran, and North Korea. Over twenty-percent of Americans are illiterate, while "Half of Americans cannot read well enough to comprehend health information," (*U.N. Sustainable Development Goals, 2019 Report.*).

Among the states, California is ranked fiftieth in literacy, with twenty-three percent of its population having <u>no</u> reading skills. That the richest state, in richest country in the world, should have such a large number of people who lack the basic ability to read and write, is almost unbelievable. That millions of potential voters cannot read election ballot materials is a social disaster.

Even fewer have the ability to write. A city teacher can have as many as one hundred and fifty student a day. There is no way to read and grade essays from that many pupils, so machine graded tests are the only way to assess a student's knowledge. Now, according to the National Assessment of Educational Statistics, the High School Writing Proficiency Test is given solely by computer (with the students allowed to use "thesaurus tools — such as "*Spell Check.*") Even so, only twenty-four percent of the students were deemed "literate."

To be considered "literate," means more than being able to read and write. True literacy opens a universe of books — literature, history, travel, the science — an infinite variety of knowledge and ideas. All were once available on library bookshelves, through which students could wander, constantly making new discoveries. There was a time when school libraries were full of students socializing--exchanging books and ideas. Now the stacks are devoid of students; if a required text is online, why bother going to the library? Even computer stations have shrunk a small areas, while students fill the cafeteria, each focused on their "Smart"-phone, or laptop.

"Literacy" once included the ability to read and write in cursive. Now, using only their thumbs to communicate, teenagers, are losing the manual dexterity to write. One survey found that sixty-percent of university undergraduates cannot read or write cursive script. As one critic found, "they are unable to read the *Declaration of Independence*, or even a birthday card from Grandma."

When the students at Martin Luther King realized that their writing would not be graded, or criticized, and would remain anonymous, they began to express their inner thoughts, needs, and aspirations, which, I believe, helped their emotional growth. Now, with the prevalence of multiple choice tests — the only way to assess a large class — there are few opportunities for students to communicate their ideas and feelings.

The isolation is often emotional and social — which leads over twenty percent of teenagers to contemplate suicide.

A Final Reflection

In reading student's papers, I was often struck by the depth of boredom and loneliness they expressed. For the most part they were interested in nothing—at least not to the point of actively pursuing an interest, particularly over a period of time. Even those most involved in drugs could seldom be persuaded to read a pamphlet or lead a discussion on the topic. There seemed to be a lack of depth, a constant reaction, rather than an initiation of movement, somewhat like a person drifting in space. Indeed, several student writing explicitly described a sense of vertigo.

Among many, there was a kind of self-destructive freedom: "If you want to shoot dope its O.K. It's my body and my mind to do with as I please." In most students it seemed that anger and hostility bubbled just beneath the surface. Outbursts in the classroom were common, pushing and threatening almost non-stop--a hostility that included parents and siblings; with home "a place to leave" as soon as possible, rather than a place of refuge.

Sadly, most parents refused to believe that their child had any emotional or behavioral problems. Always, any encounter, or class disruption, had to be the fault of another student; as their child could never be aggressive, irreligious, swear in class, be involved in dope or sex, or grappling with emotional problems. Parents constantly foisted the blame for behavioral problems at the school on other people's children. The school's dope pusher was the son of a very straight-laced mother, to whom the thought that her son had even touched a joint would have been inconceivable. The availability of marijuana was always blamed on the black students, while in fact it was used more heavily by whites, and the source was actually white dealers. One boy was growing marijuana on his back porch yet, when the parents were told, they claimed that their child, "couldn't possibly know what it is."

The same ignorance included the language their children used in everyday conversation. One mother stormed into my class because I had said "damn" in front of her daughter who, outside of mother's earshot, was the most foul-mouthed trooper imaginable.

When talking to other teachers from a number of schools, they frequently remarked, "My students are nowhere, they are not interested in lessons or studying." "They are indifferent to grades and going to college." "They are apathetic, withdrawn, and seemingly bored." "They couldn't care less about what I say or the subject matter."

This is generally true, yet, despite the negativism, many students at still seemed to possess an inner strength and optimism. For example, when asked, "If you were not you, who would you like to be?" To my surprise, superstars and sports heroes were usually ignored. Few wished to be anyone but themselves. Similarly, when given a list of possible field trips, such as to a movie, or a visit to zoo, or a TV station, most popular was simply a walk across the Golden Gate Bridge.

Looking back over my time at MLK, I find some satisfaction in the belief that, the students I had for six months, became a little more able to understand the world around them, a little more able to express their feelings and, perhaps, a little less turned off from school.

Sadly, meaningful self-expression was something few inmates of Agnews able to achieve. Some, trapped inside their schizophrenia, could sometimes verbalize their thoughts, others were truly lost. The "Emotionally Disabled" students of the Oakland Schools presented the widest array of ability, temperament, and needs, often fluctuating from moment to moment. In a way, they were the saddest group, daily teetering on the edge of mental, or physical disaster. Yet, with the right kind of help, most of these children were able to live "normal," lives. However, the limited resources of the public school system cannot provide the physical, educational, social, and emotional support such young people need, so many fall by the wayside.

―――――――――

"How beautiful it would be to fly. To float in the air and be blown by the wind." (Emily Marie).

All we need is

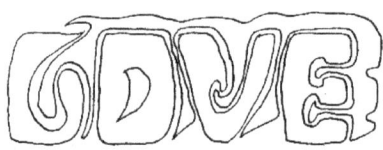

www.ingramcontent.com/pod-product-compliance
Lightning Source LLC
LaVergne TN
LVHW072021060526
838200LV00008B/221